Event Stakeholders:

Theory and Methods for Event Management and Tourism

Mathilda van Niekerk, PhD.

and Donald Getz, PhD.

(G) Goodfellow Publishers Ltd

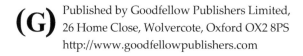 Published by Goodfellow Publishers Limited,
26 Home Close, Wolvercote, Oxford OX2 8PS
http://www.goodfellowpublishers.com

British Library Cataloguing in Publication Data: a catalogue
record for this title is available from the British Library.

Library of Congress Catalog Card Number: on file.

ISBN: 978-1-9113-9666-6

The Events Management Theory and Methods Series

 Design and typesetting by P.K. McBride, www.macbride.org.uk

Cover design by Cylinder

Printed by Baker and Taylor, www.baker-taylor.com

Contents

List of figures

List of tables

Introduction to the Events Management Theory and Methods Series

Event management as a field of study and professional practice has its textbooks with plenty of models and advice, a body of knowledge (EMBOK[1]*), competency standards (MBECS[2]**) and professional associations with their codes of conduct. But to what extent is it truly an applied management field? In other words, where is the management theory in event management, how is it being used, and what are the practical applications?

Event tourism is a related field, one that is defined by the roles events play in tourism and economic development. The primary consideration has always been economic values, although increasingly events and managed event portfolios meet more diverse goals for cities and countries for example the socio cultural values, environmental values and the increase in destination image and branding. While these aspects have been well developed, especially economic impact assessment and forecasting, the application of management theory to event tourism have not received adequate attention.

In this book series we launch a process of examining the extent to which mainstream theory is being employed to develop event-specific theory, and to influence the practice of event management and event tourism. This is a very big task, as there are numerous possible theories, models and concepts, and virtually unlimited advice available on the management of firms, small and family businesses, government agencies and not-for-profit organization. Inevitably, we will have to be selective.

The starting point is theory, not from the social or behavioral sciences - although these certainly inform management - but from the generic management literature. This encompasses theories of organization, the firm, business practice and all the commonly recognized management functions: Planning, Organizing, Staffing, Directing and Controlling. Because of EMBOK and MBECS we can add leadership, co-ordination, design, and evaluation.

Scientific theory must both explain a phenomenon, and be able to predict what will happen. Experiments are the dominant form of classical theory development. Management theory, however, is something different. Explanatory and predictive capabilities are often lacking, and it might be wiser to speak of theory in development, or theory fragments. It is often the process of theory development that marks research in management, including the testing of hypotheses and the formulation of propositions. Theory development might include comparative case studies, surveys, longitudinal research, participant observation - in short mixed methods. And some 'theories' are rather normative, reflecting what some people think should be done, rather than a description of what actually happens under given circumstances.

1 Event Management Body of Knowledge, https://www.embok.org/

2 Meetings and Business Events Competency Standards, https://www.mpiweb.org/

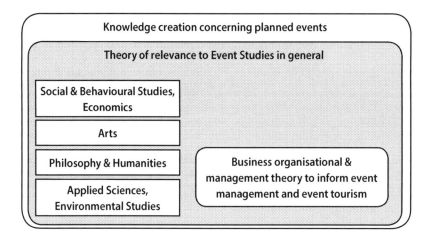

For example, when looking at stakeholder theory in detail we are not saying it explains everything nor that it can be used to predict what will happen. Rather, stakeholder theory (and many other theories) is a good starting point for understanding the real world and guiding management. There are also general principles of stakeholder management to draw upon, but managers must decide if they are applicable or if they should be modified to fit the problem. There is also normative advice, and this is always open to interpretation and debate. It should be stressed that many managers rely on problem solving skills and personal experiences to guide them, not theory. The main advantage associated with learning about stakeholder or other theories is that they are NOT situation specific. It should be possible to refer to, and use stakeholder theory in all management contexts.

All the books in this series will be relatively short, and similarly structured. They are to be used by educators who need theoretical foundations and case studies for their classes, by students in need of reference works, by professionals wanting increased understanding alongside practical methods, and by agencies or associations that want their members and stakeholders to have access to a library of valuable resources. The nature of the series is that as it grows, components can be assembled by request. That is, users can order a book or collection to exactly suit their needs.

All the books will introduce the theory, show how it is being used in the events sector through a literature review, incorporate examples and case studies written by researchers and/or practitioners, and contain methods that can be used effectively in the real world. Online resources will include annotated bibliographies, additional resources, and for educators an instructor's manual and set of power point slides.

Donald Getz, PhD

Preface to Event Stakeholders

Key objectives of the book:

- ☐ Inform researchers, students, managers, policy makers and strategists on stakeholder theory and management as applied to events and event tourism.
- ☐ Provide a comprehensive, systematic approach with methods and tools.
- ☐ Provide a textbook for students of events and tourism, and a reference for practitioners.
- ☐ Utilize case studies to illustrate key points.
- ☐ Connect readers to the research literature and encourage its consultation through use of Research Notes and provision of additional resources.

Acknowledgements

From Mathilda van Niekerk:

People surround us every day. Some people touch our lives unconscientiously and others change our lives forever. We invest a lot of resources in some of our relationships and in others a phone call once in a while is sufficient. I guess we can say that they are all stakeholders in our lives. Some primary, some secondary, some internal and some external but you will understand this more clearly as you read the book. I want to acknowledge Donald Getz who came up with the idea of the event stakeholder book and who, through the challenging times that I had to face still believed that we could complete it. To Willem Coetzee, Ubaldino Couto, Chris de Bruyn, Bekir Bora Dedeoğlu, Jacques Faul, Crystal Filep, Maksim V. Godovykh, Xin Jin, Elmarie Slabbert, Karen Weber for their contributions to the case studies. To my husband Derik van Niekerk, words cannot express how grateful I am for who you are, and for all the support, encouragement, sacrifices and patience you have shown during the last five years while I am fighting pancreatic cancer. A special thanks to my dear friend Fevzi Okumus for countless hospital visits, being my driver, laughs and being there for me and "liefie liefie" when we needed you. My family, Rosen College of Hospitality Management Family (too many to name everyone) and all my friends for all your love and support in my life. If there is anyone who understands the importance of having people 'stakeholders' in their life it is definitely me. Like a spider's web we are all woven together and to be successful everyone has a specific role to play. To be a successful event organizer in this competitive industry you need to understand this dynamic yet fragile environment and manage through it carefully. I hope the book will assist you to understand these relationships and teach you how to manage them.

From Donald Getz:

I am grateful to Mia Larson, Tommy Andersson, and Mathilda van Niekerk - researchers I have collaborated with on the subject of stakeholders and related topics. And thanks for general inspiration to Professor J.R. Brent Ritchie. Good use has been made of *Event Studies* (three editions, the third co-authored with Stephen Page) and the *Routledge Handbook of Events*, so gratitude is also expressed to Professor Stephen Page. And a special thanks to the many authors whose papers or books we have referenced, as without them there would be no body of knowledge to cite.

1 Introduction to Stakeholder Theory

Learning objectives

At the end of the chapter readers should be able to:

- ☐ Understand the meaning of shareholder and interpretations of stakeholder
- ☐ Describe the differences between internal and external stakeholders
- ☐ Describe the origins and nature of stakeholder theory
- ☐ Discuss why stakeholder theory is vital to event management and tourism
- ☐ Examine social responsibility and how it influences stakeholder management
- ☐ Differentiate between the systems theory, social network theory, collaboration theory and social exchange theory.

1.1 Introduction

Of the many management-oriented theories, concepts and models available, stakeholder theory (ST) is one of the few that has found a firm place in event management and event tourism, both in the research literature and in practice. Why? Because of the vital importance of knowing and managing stakeholders in all contexts, whether it is a single event, a city or destination, or a business dealing with events. The influence of stakeholders cannot be ignored, as they are an inherent part of planning, marketing and management.

Once you understand the basics as described in this book you should be able to identify and classify your organization or event's stakeholders and develop appropriate management tools reflecting your needs. Although the origins of the theory concern a company's external relationships, it is especially important for events and destinations to consider both internal and external stakeholders. The chapter starts with basic definitions, then goes on to fully explore stakeholder theory.

To get the reader thinking about stakeholders and their management, consider these scenarios:

1   The festival's arts director and all the artistic staff and volunteers want to change the program in substantial ways in order to attract new audiences,

but the chairperson of the board of directors (who was the founder of the festival and remains entrenched) is adamant that nothing will ever change. It is a classic case of an organizational culture conflict (I have seen this myself, and it can be messy!) and it raises issues that involve both internal stakeholders (staff, volunteers, directors) and external stakeholders – especially those bodies giving financial support to the festival who want it to become more financially sustainable. How is it to be resolved?

2   A member-based destination marketing organization (DMO) is developing and marketing an event portfolio to maximize tourism and other economic benefits for the city, but some of the events it wants to promote and grow are funded and coordinated within the city's arts and culture department. In fact, cities and destinations often have multiple portfolios of events pertaining to separate policy fields such as tourism, arts, culture, sport, health or leisure. How do all these stakeholders (some businesses, others local government, still others not-for-profits) agree on goals and strategy? Who is responsible for bringing them together and working towards consensus?

3   An international sport governing body owns the rights to host a popular event that is in high demand, and so it obtains many concessions and large bidding fees from cities or countries that want the event. The event owners have power, at least up to the point where the rights to host the event are granted, then the organizers have the obligation to get it done. Relationships between stakeholders often involve unbalanced power relationships, questions of legitimacy (i.e., who should be involved or consulted) and an inequitable distribution of benefits and costs.

These scenarios illustrate some of the important stakeholder-related challenges within event and tourism management. Scenario 1 involves mostly internal stakeholders in a power struggle, but most event organizations cannot isolate their decisions from the influence of, or impacts on external stakeholders. In scenario 2 diverse stakeholders must find a way to cooperate and work towards common goals – a challenge requiring diplomacy and leadership that most leaders face, and in a variety of situations. The third scenario introduces the inevitable challenges related to legitimacy, power and consequences when managing stakeholder relationships – challenges played out over and over in many different settings.

In this book we examine stakeholder theory as it relates to event and tourism management, with emphasis on demonstrating both challenges and applications. The ultimate aim of this book, and the entire series, is to position these applied fields more firmly within the management mainstream. This does not mean the *business* mainstream, as governmental and not-for-profit perspectives are just as important. Our approach takes into account the unique aspects of tourism and events management that requires adaptation of mainstream management theory and methods.

1.2 Key terms defined

The term 'stakeholder' is now in common use, but not always mentioned with regard to underlying theory. The purpose of theory is to provide general knowledge that can be applied in any situation, based on research and discourse. Of importance is the fact that people define stakeholders in different ways, and it keeps evolving. Once you understand the basics as described in this book you should feel free to identify and classify your organization or event's stakeholders and develop appropriate management tools reflecting your needs.

Note that there are two definitions of stakeholder from Freeman, reflecting the evolution of thinking about this subject. Although the origins of the theory concern a private company's external relationships, it is especially important for events and destinations to consider both internal and external stakeholders.

To hold a 'stake' in something is to make an investment, as reflected in the old term 'grubstakes' which was applied to the investment people made in an enterprise (like gold mining) in return for a share of any profits. Of course, the grubstake could also have been completely lost. Nowadays, one's stake in an event or in tourism could be emotional or political, with perceived legitimacy being a key determinant.

Freeman (2004) defined stakeholders as those groups who are vital to survival or success. He said stakeholder theory leads to managers articulating who are their key stakeholders, how they can create value working together, and how they can be brought together. The theory can help managers be more effective in negotiating with stakeholders. This view of stakeholder theory emphasizes practical considerations important to all business managers.

There are four general perspectives on stakeholder theory, discussed fully in Chapter 2: descriptive or empirical (exploring how organizations work in a stakeholder environment); instrumental (determination of how stakeholder relationships and their management actually affect the organization and achievement of its goals); managerial (theory development leading to recommended practices, attitudes, structures for stakeholder management); and normative.

The normative approach to stakeholder theory stresses ethics, including the principle of corporate social responsibility (CSR). It admonishes that companies should not be solely inward looking, and that they cannot simply focus on maximizing profit for owners and shareholders. This is in part rooted in philosophy, and in part based on strategy – the belief that organizations must be responsive and open.

Freeman (1984, p. 40) said this about social responsibility:

> *"While there have been many criticisms of the research in corporate social responsibility, perhaps the most troubling issue is the very nature of 'corporate social responsibility' as if the concept were needed to augment the study of business*

policy... We need to understand the complex interconnections between economic and social forces. Isolating 'social issues' as separate from the economic impact, which they have, and conversely isolating economic issues as if they had no social effect, misses the mark both managerially and intellectually. Actions aimed at one side will not address the concerns of the other. Processes, techniques and theories that do not consider all of these forces will fail to describe and predict the business world as it really is."

Not all adherents of stakeholder theory believe it involves CSR or ethics. The original perspective was that of business managers who traditionally only took into account the interests of owners and/or shareholders. However, the normative position (i.e. value-based) on stakeholder theory is that *business ethics* and *social responsibility* should be part of every organization's mandate.

We can make the definition for stakeholder theory more suitable for events and tourism, and in these contexts it is considered to be essential to encompass the twin notions of ethical relationships and social responsibility. Let us look at the following key concepts and definitions:

Stakeholder

"Any individual or group who can affect the firm's performance or who is affected by the achievement of the organization's objectives" (Freeman, 1984) or "those groups who are vital to the survival and success of the corporation" (Freeman, 2004). Carroll (1993) defines stakeholders as "those groups or individuals with whom the organization interacts or has interdependencies" or Savage et al. (1991) describe them as "groups or individuals who have an interest in the actions of an organization and ... the ability to influence it."

Internal stakeholders

Those persons and groups involved in the organization itself, or within the event, including staff, volunteers, directors/owners and key advisers; co-producers of events might be included here, such as occurs when various organizations combine their efforts to produce an event, or at the destination level it arises through inter-company marketing collaborations.

External stakeholders

Those external to the organization or event, including community, suppliers, regulators, supporters and partners, lobby groups, and the public at large. The existing audience and target market segments are crucial external stakeholders, as are the media, politicians and possibly other events – even if they are potential competitors.

Shareholder

"A shareholder is any person, company or other institution that owns at least one share of a company's stock. Because shareholders are a company's owners, they reap

the benefits of the company's successes in the form of increased stock valuation...
Also unlike the leadership of other business types, companies with shareholders rely
on a board of directors and executive management to run things — meaning the
actual owners, the shareholders, don't have much say in the day-to-day operation of
the business...A shareholder may also be referred to as a stockholder" Investopdia
(2018).

Stakeholder theory (ST)

"A conceptual framework of business ethics and organizational management
which addresses moral and ethical values in the management of a business or
other organization. The stakeholder theory was first proposed in the book Strategic Management: A Stakeholder Approach *by R. Edward Freeman and out-*
lines how management can satisfy the interests of stakeholders in a business."
WebFinance (2018).

Stakeholder theory for events

Stakeholder theory is a conceptual framework and set of propositions regarding
why and how events and tourism organizations should involve and manage
internal and external stakeholders, in an ethical and socially responsible manner.

System theory

"Systems theory or systems science is the interdisciplinary study of systems. A
system is an entity with interrelated and interdependent parts; it is defined by its
boundaries and it is more than the sum of its parts (subsystem). Change in one part
of the system affects other parts and the whole system, with predictable patterns of
behavior. Positive growth and adaptation of a system depend upon how well the
system is adjusted with its environment, and systems often exist to accomplish a
common purpose." Wikipedia (2018a).

Social network theory

"A social network is a social structure made up of a set of social actors (such
as individuals or organizations), sets of dyadic ties, and other social interactions
between actors. The social network perspective provides a set of methods for analyz-
ing the structure of whole social entities as well as a variety of theories explaining
the patterns observed in these structures." Wikipedia (2018b).

Collaboration theory

Collaboration can be investigated from an interorganizational, intraorganiza-
tional or interpersonal level. It can be defined as collaborative interactions or
influence tactic for garnering cooperation (Yukl, Chavez and Seifert, 2005). It
encompasses how collaboration works irrespective of the level and structure it
takes place in (Colbry, Hurwitz and Adair, 2014).

Social exchange theory

"Social exchange theory is a social psychological and sociological perspective that explains social change and stability as a process of negotiated exchanges between parties. Social exchange theory posits that human relationships are formed by the use of a subjective cost-benefit analysis and the comparison of alternatives. The theory has roots in economics, psychology and sociology. Social exchange theory features many of the main assumptions found in rational choice theory and structuralism. It is also used quite frequently in the business world to imply a two-sided, mutually contingent and rewarding process involving transactions or simply exchange." Wikipedia (2018c)

1.3   Case Study - The Octagon Experience, New Zealand

Willem Coetzee, University of Otago, New Zealand
Crystal Filep, University of Otago, New Zealand

City context: Dunedin with a population of 120,000 people is the second largest city on the South Island of New Zealand. When Ed Sheeran announced that he would be performing in the city, the first two concerts of 40,000 tickets each sold out within minutes and the organizers had to book a third show. In total 115,000 people attended the shows, and close to 70,000 visitors helped to generate an estimated NZ$34 million into the local economy. For a city of this size these figures are substantial, and the Dunedin City Council (DCC) realized the potential. As part of the festivities the DCC's urban design team organized a fan-zone in the central public space, or plaza, of Dunedin known as The Octagon. Dr. Filep and her team designed a fringe, temporary placemaking event for five days while Ed Sheeran was in town, and they called it The Octagon Experience. Normally dominated by vehicular uses, the lower half of The Octagon was temporarily pedestrianized and activated to create a central hub in which concert goers and other members of the public could socialize and create memorable experiences.

Type of event: The Octagon Experience was a temporary pedestrianisation / activation of urban space to create a 'central hub' for residents and visitors.

Different stakeholders for the event

Events cross political and departmental boundaries to have an impact upon social, environmental and economic environments, including but not limited to education, place making, economic development and employment. With a number of visitors to the city, DCC's urban designers saw an opportunity and convinced management to also use the event to explore placemaking possibilities. Due to the fact that The Octagon Experience took place in the city's central public space, a number of stakeholders were affected and had an interest in the area and the event. Wood (2006) describes such interest as "defin[ing] perceptions of the place"; local officials, business leaders and residents believe that they should have a say in various aspects of the event that may impact them. The event experience is always at least partially dependent upon the expectations and attitudes of stakeholders. For The Octagon Experience it was important for the event organizer to identify the stakeholders and to motivate them to "enter into the spirit of the occasion" (Getz and Page, 2016:245). In order to gain support for The Octagon Experience, Dr. Filep and her team had to negotiate with stakeholders within the Dunedin City Council as well as the external stakeholders. The following is a reflection about stakeholder engagement.

Internal to Dunedin City Council (DCC)

Most of the internal stakeholders ensured compliance with regulations, but they also made sure that the event ran safely and effectively within a healthy environment.

◆ Executive Leadership Team (ELT) of the local government, who have the authority to sign-off on (or reject) project ideas and implementation details.

◆ Community Development Department, including the DCC's Event Management Team.

◆ Enterprise Dunedin, who are responsible for economic development and tourism, and who oversaw the wider visit of Ed Sheeran to Dunedin.

◆ Parks & Recreation Department, who advised on temporary planting, helped with temporary storage needs, is also the department responsible for the management of The Octagon; the event organizers (urban design team) had to book The Octagon through the Parks & Recreation Department as a 'sports field booking', even though it is a public urban plaza.

◆ Resource Consent Team, who ensured that environmental resources were protected during the event; the event organizers had to apply for Resource Consent for signage and artwork used during the event.

◆ Transport Department, who process applications for temporary road closures and are responsible for the maintenance of Dunedin's road infrastructure; the event organizers had to submit a temporary road closure application to the Transport Department for the event.

◆ Health & Safety Team, who reviewed the event's Health & Safety Plan and ensured that all contractors used during the event were 'approved' within the DCC system.

◆ Solid Waste Department, who organized additional waste removal and recycling resources during the event.

◆ The Liquor Licensing Team, who ensured that the event took place within limits of the local government's liquor license policy.

External to the DCC:

Affected parties (ownership/tenancy of immediate property or business)

♦ Property owners around the plaza

♦ Property tenants such as business owners as well as residents living in residential lofts around the plaza

Health & Safety

♦ New Zealand Police/Nga Pirihimana O Aotearoa

♦ Fire and Emergency New Zealand

♦ St John New Zealand (ambulance)

♦ Disabilities Information Action Group

Operational

♦ Volunteers

  ❖ Task Force Green, whohelped manufacture some furniture and with event set-up/take-down.

  ❖ The 'yarn bombers', which is a community initiative of a group of people that supplied knitted pieces, such as cushions and décor to create a true New Zealand experience using wool and local handicraft. As part of this initiative local wool suppliers and knitting groups such as Knitworld, Gasworks Spinners and Weavers as well as church groups such as Presbyterian Support group contributed.

  ❖ Core sponsors as suppliers of building material at reduced rate included two local hardware stores, Bunnings Warehouse and Mitre 10 MEGA.

♦ Paid contractors employed by the DCC team:

  ❖ Traffic Management & Control Ltd

  ❖ Allied Security (during event)

  ❖ North Dunedin Bloke Shed (manufacture of 'pallet furniture')

  ❖ Hall Bros (deliver of 'pallet furniture')

  ❖ Network Visuals (installation of lighting and lanterns)

  ❖ Dakins Group (supply & servicing of port-a-loos)

  ❖ Visionary Digital (supply of 'chutes + ladders' board)

  ❖ Williams Signs + Graphix (installation of 'chutes + ladders' board)

  ❖ Trees of the World (supply of movable trees/planters)

  ❖ Hirepool (forklift supply)

  ❖ Delta (forklift operator)

  ❖ Touchscreen Marketing & Research (questionnaires)

- Other operators during event included
  - ❖ Otago Regional Council (bus operations / stops)
  - ❖ My Little Local, a local information App.
  - ❖ Taxi operators
  - ❖ Food vendors such as Dinkum Donuts, Artisan State Coffee, Fudi, Out and About and St Mary's School BBQ
  - ❖ Dunedin Midwinter Carnival (Autumn Lights in The Athenaeum)
  - ❖ local artists (interactive 'paint by numbers' Ed Sheeran mural)
  - ❖ 1100 kids playing ukuleles (with teachers / chaperones)
  - ❖ young local musicians: Painted Blind, Bark Like a Dog)
  - ❖ Ed Sheeran 'pop-up hub' (sale of fan merchandise)

Photo 1.1: 1100 local children playing ukuleles. Picture credit: Author's own C. Filep.

What was the process used to identify the stakeholders?

External stakeholders were identified as those immediately adjacent and therefore potentially affected by the event area, those who were essential in terms of addressing health and safety matters, and those who were operating in the area during the event (either by their own initiative or as initiated by our team).

Was one stakeholder group more important than others? Why?

All stakeholder groups were essential. Engagement with the Affected Parties (ownership / tenancy of immediate property or business) could be considered the 'most important', as this group of ratepayers and contributors to the city center could make or break the event, and have complex operational needs / concerns. Their signatures were also essential for approval of the Traffic Management Plan.

How did you involve the stakeholders?

As a general rule of thumb, we engaged the stakeholders through repeated interactions and through multiple means (especially the Affected Parties). For the Affected Parties, this involved an initial phone call and/or email from a City Planning administrator, then an in-person visit / chat from myself (Team Leader Urban Design) and DCC Enterprise Dunedin Business Relationship Manager with information sheets and signature forms. During these visits / chats, personal attention and following up of queries became very important. Follow-up questionnaires were also distributed to Affected Parties for post-event feedback.

Photo 1.2: Giant snakes-and-ladders. Picture credit: Author's own C. Filep.

Any problems with any of the stakeholders?

Two business owners (of Sue Todd Antiques and Seriously Twisted Ltd) in particular were staunchly opposed to the temporary road closure/pedestrianisation of The Octagon. Their views are summarized the local media piece (Lewis, 2018): https://www.odt.co.nz/news/dunedin/central-hub-concert-weekend

Was there a specific focus on the local community where the event took place?

A driving idea behind The Octagon Experience was to celebrate the city in a way that appealed to visitors and also gave back to locals. Public feedback reported to the DCC's Planning and Environment Committee on 17 April 2018 suggests that the local community was proud of the event and saw it as a positive temporary transformation of the city center. Some of the comments related to the overall experience and atmosphere: "It was AWESOME!! We are Dunedin locals and we loved soaking up the atmosphere in the Octagon. Loved all the added things to do in the Octagon and the lawn furniture and decorations."

The creative energy and overall vibe of the events was also viewed in a positive view: "People were out having fun everywhere you looked. The street plantings and outdoor furniture was pretty. My son loved the snakes and ladders game. It would be awesome to have games like that all the time. Especially if the board could rotate a couple of different games each month. I liked the street being closed to traffic. It is quieter, smelled better for those eating outdoors, and is just more enjoyable."

A closure of some road were initially not embraced, but during the events attendees commented that: "I'd like to see motor vehicles out of the Octagon altogether". Some even recommended that this should be a permanent feature: "I'm confused why it's not closed like this all the time. I'm struggling to think of another city that has traffic going through its main hub. Traffic is hardly put out by it being closed."

As part of a tourism offering one participant commented that: "I would love to see this as a permanent feature of Dunedin. It is great place for locals and really great for tourists to enjoy." "The ease of access in a space that is clearly focusing around pedestrian usage. It felt natural and was an absolute pleasure to recreate in the octagon while unnecessary traffic passed by on the other streets."

The DCC team and stakeholders involved received commendations, such as: "I am not a fan of Ed Sheeran but I applaud the DCC and how they handled such an opportunity – Dunedin as a destination. My hat is off to everyone involved." Some of the participants compared it to other international event-full cities: "Many of us have asked for a car free central city for years where other cities have these zones they are a huge success, e.g. Cuba St Wellington, it brings more business and life to the city, not less".

Place making and public spaces are important for local well-being and it is important that we safeguard these public spaces for local residents. One participant mentioned that "Cities are defined by their public hubs, Martin Place and Circular Quay in Sydney are great examples. It's nice to close the ring road around the lower Octagon from time to time and feel like a modern city...without the overcrowding!" Another made a similar comment: "It's great to have these things set up for tourists and events, but what about those of us who live here? Many cities worldwide have car-free zones and businesses and residents all benefit. Let's do it here and make Dunedin awesome for those of us who live here, and not just for fans."

How did you manage the stakeholders?

Stakeholders were managed via the involvement approach mentioned above and through detailed spreadsheets documenting these interactions and any related actions arising.

Lessons learned from the stakeholder engagement

The key lesson learned was that stakeholder engagement is essential to get right. My team was complemented for our work in this regard, as we went 'above and beyond' what the DCC typically does (partially due to our inexperience of event planning – we are urban designers and landscape architects, and partially because of upper management's risk-adverse stance due to Ed Sheeran's high profile). What was surprising was the lack of an established system (including a list of names and contact info, order of essential engagement steps, etc.) that we could use to help guide us through the engagement process. Although many events / road closures happen in The Octagon, my team was given very little information to work with and had to 'reinvent the wheel'. A lot of unnecessary time, energy and stress could be avoided if a system is established and re-used / adapted for similar events / road closures happening in a particular place or condition.

1.4   Historical development of stakeholder theory

Freeman (1984) is widely credited with popularizing stakeholder theory, but his treatise had foundations. His acknowledged intellectual origins included strategic organizational planning, systems theory and organization theory. Australian event researchers Sasha Reid and Charles Arcodia wrote a paper in 2002 that serves as a good overview. In fact, this paper was most likely the earliest event-specific, in-depth discussion of stakeholder theory.

Reid, S., & Arcodia, C. (2002). Understanding the role of the stakeholder in event management.

> "Stakeholder theory emerged in the early 1960s with the Stanford Research Institute discussing the role of stakeholders in supporting the activities of an organization. Ansoff (1965) further explained that balancing the conflicting claims of these various stakeholders should determine the objectives of an organization. Previous to this, the view was that the initiatives and thoughts of stakeholders were external to the strategic planning and management processes of organizations (Dill, 1975). Stakeholder theory proposes that in a competitive business environment there are other factors that contribute to an organization's success apart from the attainment of profits. One of the key principles of stakeholder theory is that an organization is granted license to operate by virtue of its social contract with stakeholders (Robson & Robson, 1996). If society sees a benefit in an organization's activity, it will continue to allow the organization to operate.

The term *stakeholder* came into the tourism literature in the 1970s, much earlier than in the events field where it was not widely used (if at all) until the 1990s. The classic 1978 paper by Heenan, *Tourism and the Community - A Drama in Three Acts*, mentioned stakeholder legitimacy when examining host-community attitudes towards hallmark events, and that might be the earliest example of relevance to both tourism and event management (Heenan, 1978). Chacko and Shaffer (1993) called for stakeholder involvement in festival and event planning. Getz & Jamal (1994) and Jamal and Getz (1995) emphasized stakeholders within the frame collaboration theory while studying community-based tourism planning.

A deeper examination of the literature reveals that constructs closely related to stakeholder theory have also been guiding event and tourism research. Event management research and theorizing by Getz and Frisby (1988) and Frisby and Getz (1989) touched upon basic stakeholder issues in the context of how community festivals were managed, and issues related to their evolution or professionalization, without actually using the term stakeholder. Systems theory was employed, resulting in a model of the event management system, and with systems approaches to tourism and events there is always direct acknowledgement of interdependences. Indeed, *systems theory* holds that all organizations are dependent upon the wider environment for necessary resources and support. The 'political market square' has been used as a concept for examining event management by Larson and Wikstrom (2001) and Larson (2002, 2009), and is founded in organizational and collaboration theory and stresses legitimacy building – a key element in stakeholder theory.

Editors Chappelet and Parent (2015) discussed stakeholder theory and its relevance in the introductory chapter to the *Routledge Handbook of Sports Event Management*. They also commented upon the nature of management 'theory', saying (p. 14) of stakeholder theory that it is a 'framework' that helped organize the handbook, but it does not provide an integrated set of testable hypotheses or propositions. That is generally the nature of all management theory, and it is a position supported by the experts on organizational ecology (Hannan et. al. 2007) who described it as a set of 'theory fragments'. In other words, management theories in general are not explanatory and predictive, and most of the pertinent literature can be considered as theory in development.

In Table 1.1 are a series of quotes, in chronological order, indicating important uses of the terms stakeholder and stakeholder theory, and closely related terms and concepts, from the events and tourism literature. The use of stakeholder theory has increased steadily so that now it is an accepted and important construct and set of management principles for event and tourism applications. Indeed, the literature is too vast to completely document all the ways stakeholder theory is employed.

Table 1.1: How 'stakeholder' and related terms have been used in the events and tourism literature (N.B. italics have been added by the authors to emphasize key concepts)

Heenan, 1978. P. 30: "Legitimacy refers to *stakeholder* perceptions that the institution deserves to exist. This occurs, for instance, only when locals believe that the firm's investment in the visitor industry is essential in promoting the social and economic wellbeing of their community. Since legitimacy is confirmed not by management, but rather by outside or external *stakeholders*, the future of tourism in many parts of the world will be determined as much for legitimacy reasons as for viability."

Chacko and Shaffer, 1993, p. 482: "Several lessons can be learned from the Creole Christmas case, as new special events and festivals are developed in urban communities:

• Use and build a festival around existing heritage and cultural resources that provide an authentic and credible *marketing foundation*.

• A core group of *activists,* consisting of major *stakeholders*, must be involved from the outset.

Getz and Jamal, 1994, p. 152: " This article advances the proposition that *sustainable tourism* can be achieved through recognition that the public and private sector, the host communities and the natural environment are interdependent *stakeholders* in a complex *tourism 'domain',* where no single individual, agency or group can resolve strategic tourism issues by acting alone."

Jamal and Getz, 1995, p. 188. "Based on an examination of the literature and adapting Gray's (1989) definition, the authors posit that *collaboration* for community-based tourism planning is a process of *joint decision- making* among autonomous, key *stakeholders* of an inter-organizational, community tourism domain to resolve planning problems of the domain and/or to manage issues related to the planning and development of the domain."

Larson and Wikstrom, 2001, p. 52: "A political perspective, in the analysis of relational interaction in a *project network* marketing an event, has led to the introduction of a metaphor for a project network, the *Political Market Square* (Larson, 1997, 2000). The metaphor emphasizes the structure of the event project network as an open arena for loosely and tightly coupled *actors* to act and interact upon. Some actors are central, whereas others are peripheral in the Market Square. The actors engage themselves in the event in order to further their own interests. Therefore, political processes are present within the relationships between actors."

Sheehan and Ritchie, 2005, p.711: This paper explores "…the potential of using *stakeholder theory* as a foundation of *strategic tourism destination management*. A major outcome of the study is an empirical identification of the *major players* of a typical tourism destination and a determination of their relative salience to the DMO, as well as their perceived ability to threaten and cooperate with the organizations."

Getz, Andersson and Larson, 2007, p. 104: "In terms of *resource dependency theory*, event managers must be effective in managing *stakeholders* in order to occupy a permanent, supportive *niche* in the community."

d'Angella and Go, 2009. "This paper focuses on *collaborative tourism marketing* practice, particularly the relationship between the Destination Management Organization (DMO) and tourism firms. It applies *stakeholder theory* as a framework for such performance assessment concerning the capability of a DMO to gain support for decision making, which contributes towards optimizing stakeholders' rewards while minimizing risks."

Larson, 2009, p. 394. "Larson (2002) found that in recurring events some of the *actors in the event network* are present every year, whereas some only occasionally and others only once. The event organizer can be regarded as the *actor* having the strongest power position, based on *legitimized* authority to include and exclude *stakeholders*."

Chappelet and Parent, 2015, p. 14. "This Handbook [Routledge Handbook of Sports Event Management] addresses the descriptive approach presenting chapters focused on each of the main stakeholder groups. It addresses the instrumental approach through presenting the impacts of a given stakeholder on sport events' outcome/performance. Finally, it addresses the normative aspect through presenting issues of sustainability, CSR, green initiatives, legacy, and /or leveraging associated with the stakeholder being analyzed."

Van Niekerk, 2016. "Several tourism and festival studies have used the *stakeholder theory* in their research. Most of this research tended to focus on the identification of destination and festival stakeholders (Garrod et al., 2012; Andersson & Getz, 2009; Getz et al., 2007; Larson, 2002; Reid & Arcodia, 2002; Sheehan & Ritchie, 2005; van Niekerk, 2014) while others focused on the roles and functions of these stakeholders (Anuar, Ahmad, Jusoh, & Hussain, 2012; Getz et al., 2007; Karlsen & Nordstrom, 2009). Very few studies have, however, explored the management strategies of destination and festival stakeholders.

Research note

Byrd, E. (2007). Stakeholders in sustainable tourism development and their roles: Applying stakeholder theory to sustainable tourism development. *Tourism Review*, **62** (2), 6-13.

Abstract: Sustainability has become an important topic and concept in relation to tourism planning and development. For sustainable tourism development to be successful stakeholders must be involved in the process. The questions that should be considered though are: (1) who should be considered stakeholders in tourism development, and (2) how should planners and developers involve stakeholders in the development of tourism? In order to provide answers to these questions this paper investigated sustainable tourism development and how stakeholder inclusion and involvement are incorporated in the basic concept of sustainable tourism development. This investigation was accomplished by reviewing and drawing conclusions from the literature. The discussion includes thoughts from both management and public participation perspectives. So who should be involved in the sustainable tourism development process? Based on the definitions that are used for sustainability and sustainable tourism four distinct groups are identified; the present visitors, future visitors, present host community, and future host community.

Keywords: Stakeholder theory, sustainable tourism, community participation, tourism policy

1.5 The relevance of other theories

Stakeholder theory has both foundations in, and links with other prevalent management and organizational theories. In this section an overview is provided of systems, collaboration, social network and social exchange theories, with examples from the events and tourism literature. Figure 1.1 illustrates some of the key elements that provide a more complete understanding of organizations and their interactions. These apply to individuals as well, but that is not the focus of this book.

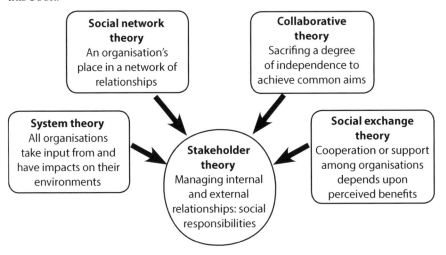

Figure 1.1: The relevance of other theories to the stakeholder theory. Source: Authors' contribution

1.5.1 Systems theory

The competitive position of a firm, or even the viability of an organization, might very well depend upon maintaining favorable relations with multiple stakeholders, not the least of which are those providing funds and other support (the facilitators), suppliers and allies. In systems theory no organization can stand alone, but must interact constantly with its immediate environment (usually the local government area and proximal institutions) and pay attention to broader forces and trends in the wider environment. Everything the event or tourism agency does has impacts, and they are always open to external evaluation. Musgrave and Woodward (2016) explained general systems theory and the need for managers and planners to engage in 'systems thinking'. They used the term 'ecological systems theory' in a particular way while focusing on social responsibility.

Research note

Musgrave, J., & Woodward, S. (2016). Ecological systems theory approach to corporate social responsibility: Contextual perspectives from meeting planners. *Event Management, 20,* 365–381.

Abstract: Business reputation, competitive advantage, differentiation, and regulatory adherence are all factors that are pushing corporate social responsibility (CSR) center stage within the international meetings industry. However, attempts to simplify what is essentially a complex and contextual driven movement through certification and guides has created an incomplete understanding of the salient issues; contemporaneously ignoring contextual variables rather than acknowledging these and the impact these variables have on CSR practice and acceptance. The purpose of this article is to explore the contextual debate of CSR adaptation and practice within the meetings sector within a framework of an ecological systems theory. The authors applied a constant comparison process across 90 interview transcripts in order to establish a rigorous audit trail of analysis. Eight practices were identified: Green Technology, Legislation, Transparency and Reliability, Nonfinancial Donations, Workforce, Community Engagement, Supply Chain Management, and Volunteer Labour. These eight practices were then applied to the constructs of an ecological systems model and an exploration of contextual factors was considered. In recognizing a systems approach to CSR there is an acceptance that there is not one best method and that different values, implementation approaches, and evaluation mechanisms of CSR can lead to similar results.

Keywords: Corporate social responsibility (CSR); context; meeting planners; ecological systems theory; events management

1.5.2 Social network theory

Systems theory provides a strong foundation for stakeholder theory, and social network theory provides a framework for analyzing stakeholder interactions. While there are many dyadic ties (i.e., one on one) between stakeholders, some being more critical than others, organizations, like people, have multiple links that form potentially complex networks. Examining these networks can help identify the sources of influence and power, competitive advantage, new opportunities, and threats from the environment. Organizations with centrality in dense networks can have multiple advantages in the flow of information, support, and resource acquisition, while those at the periphery, with few links, might very well be permanently disadvantaged. For periodic events, this suggests that fostering stakeholder relationships and getting into dense inter-organizational networks is a must for long-term viability. One-time events will likely have to rely on existing networks that led to the bid or creation in the first place.

'Holes' or gaps occur in networks where there are 'weak ties' or no 'bridges' connecting actors or clusters within networks, and these have to be filled. An isolated festival or cluster of events, lacking close ties to tourism or local government, for example, will likely experience problems. Network analysis identifies holes, leading to action to fill the gaps.

Several papers are cited below that employed social network analysis. The Ziakas and Costa article (2010) is a good example of network analysis in the community events sector, and also introduces collaboration and event portfolios. The article by Van Niekerk (2014) explores tourism destination networks and suggests stakeholder management strategies. Jarman et al. (2014) used social network analysis in the context of Edinburgh's festivals, while Booth (2016) focused on production networks and introduced the concept of 'network society'. Izzo, Bonetti, and Masiello (2012) identified the role of 'network orchestrator' and differences between the 'core network' marked by "very strong ties, defined by high degrees of intimacy, familiarity and trust" and the 'extended network' involving only occasional stakeholders with weak ties.

Research notes

Ziakas, V., and Costa, C. (2010). Explicating inter-organizational linkages of a host community's events network. *International Journal of Event and Festival Management*, **1** (2), 132-147.

From the abstract: "The purpose of this paper is to examine the inter-organizational patterns of an events network that shape a host community's capacity to capitalize on its event portfolio. ... Results showed that collaboration was not consistent across all types of links. The most central organizations in the network were the Tourism Department and the Chamber. Shared information was the predominant type of link with other types of links being weaker resulting in low multiplexity scores. Reciprocity among existing links was above average. Finally, the organizations appeared to have high levels of trust and positive attitudes toward collaboration."

Keywords: Calendar events, networking

Van Niekerk, M. (2014). The role of the public sector in tourism destination management from a network relationship approach. *Tourism Analysis*, **19**, 701–718.

Abstract: The study aims to determine the suitability of the dyadic approach and the network relationship approach when engaging destination stakeholders and to identify the roles of the public sector within destination management. These aims are investigated in the context of Mbombela Local Municipality, South Africa. A conceptual framework was developed based on a literature review. Data were then collected through official documents, 55 semi structured interviews with key stakeholders, a local economic summit, forum discussions, and 504 demand- and 403 supply-side questionnaires. The study findings suggest that the network relationship approach was the most suitable approach for the engagement of destination stakeholders. In addition to the roles identified in previous studies, the study findings identified several additional roles that the public sector should fulfill in destination management. Based on the findings, a new conceptual framework for the role of the public sector in destination management has been proposed. By utilizing the conceptual framework developed in this study, destinations can engage their stakeholders more effectively and increase the attractiveness of their destinations. This is one of a few studies from Africa providing empirical findings on destination management and the role of the public sector within destination management.

Keywords: Destination management; roles of public sector; network relationship approach; stakeholder theory

Jarman, D., Theodoraki, E., Hall, H. & Ali-Knight, J. (2014). Social network analysis and festival cities: An exploration of concepts, literature and methods. *International Journal of Event & Festival Management,* **5**(3), 311-322.

Abstract: *Purpose* – Social network analysis (SNA) is an under-utilized framework for research into festivals and events. The purpose of this paper is to reflect on the history of SNA and explore its key concepts, in order that they might be applied to festivals and their environments.

Design/methodology/approach – Secondary material underpins the paper, primarily SNA literature, tourism studies research and festival industry publications.

Findings – Festival cities offer dynamic environments in which to investigate the workings of social networks. The importance of these has long been recognized within the industry, yet there is scant reflection of this in the event studies literature . Uses of SNA in tourism studies publications offer some precedents.

Originality/value – This paper emphasizes the importance of relationships between people in a festival economy, complementing and building upon stakeholder analyses. A research method is proposed, suitable for application across a diverse range of festivals and events.

Keywords: Social media, tourism, social network analysis, festivals, Edinburgh

Booth, A. (2016). Negotiating diasporic culture: Festival collaborations and production networks. *International Journal of Event and Festival Management,* **7** (2), 100 - 116.

Abstract: *Purpose* – Within New Zealand, cultural festivals play a vital role in the local representation of diasporic cultures. By analyzing the production design of festivals, in Auckland, New Zealand representing Indian culture between 1995 and 2015, the purpose of this paper is to create a deeper understanding of collaborative networks and power relationships. Using Richard's pulsar/iterative network theory and Booth's notion of cultural production networks, a new theoretical model is proposed to visually track the collaborative networks that sustain and bridge cultures, empower communities and fulfil political agendas.

Design/methodology/approach – This ethnographic research draws upon event management studies, industry practice, ethnomusicology and sociology to take a multi-disciplinary approach to an applied research project. Using Richards' pulsar and iterative event framework Castells' network theory, combined with qualitative data, this research considers critical collaborative relationships clusters and how they might impact on the temporal nature of festivals.

Findings – The 1997 Festival of Asia and the subsequent Lantern Festival in 2000 and Diwali: Festival of Lights in 2002 were pulsar events that played a significant role in collaborative networks that expand across cultures, countries and traditions. The subsequent iterative events have played a vital role in the representation of Asian cultural identity in general and, more specifically, representing of the city's growing – in both size and cultural diversity – Indian diaspora.

Originality/value – This research proposes a new conceptual model on festival management and diasporic communities in the Asia-Pacific region. Richards' and Booth's conceptual models are used, as a starting point, to offer a new way of considering the importance of looking at collaborative relationships through historical perspectives. The framework explored contributes a new approach to cultural festival network theory and a means to understand the complexity of networks required that engage actors from inside and outside both local and global communities.

Keywords: New Zealand, Production networks, cultural festivals, Indian diaspora, pulsar and iterative events.

Izzo, F., Bonetti, E., & Masiello, B. (2012). Strong ties within cultural organization event networks and local development in a tale of three festivals. *Event Management*, **16**, 223–244.

Abstract: The purpose of this article is to provide a deeper understanding of successful event networks and offer a conceptual framework which can be used to analyze their impact on local development. In particular, this study addresses two research questions. First, how does network structure affect the success of the event and its outcomes on local development, other than in economic terms? Second, which main capabilities does the 'network orchestrator' need to promote the effectiveness of the event network? By analyzing three different Italian cultural festivals – *Festivaletteratura* ('Festival of Literature', Mantua), *Festival della Scienza* ('Festival of Science', Genoa), and *Festivalfil-osofia* ('Festival of Philosophy', Modena, Carpi, Sassuolo)—this article sheds light on: (a) the features of successful event networks, (b) the dynamics linking network structure and the social outcomes generated, and (c) the typical bundle of relational capabilities that network orchestrators need. Then we draw some implications for management and offer some remarks to stimulate further research in the field of special events.

Keywords: Festival and special events; event management; local development; network theory

Network society

Castells (2009, 2011) argued that information technology, globalization, and new forms of organization networking have led to a 'network society'. Individuals easily get organized through social networks (facilitated by social media), while businesses must usually work at both global and local levels, with the dominant forces being global in nature. Richards (2015) applied the concept to events, saying "From this viewpoint, events can play an important role in creating and circulating the cultural codes and content produced by local programmers in the network society, and therefore play an important role in the representation of places." Richards (see the abstract) also introduces the differences between 'pulsar' and 'iterative' events in this context.

Research note

Richards, G. (2015). Events in the network society: The role of pulsar and iterative events. *Event Management*, **19**, 553–566.

Abstract: This conceptual article argues for a broader view of the role of events in social systems. When analyzed as social phenomena, events can be seen as social actors that have the potential to both sustain and transform social systems. The maintenance of social systems is often reliant on iterative events, regularly occurring celebrations that tend to confirm social structures. In contrast, pulsar events have the potential to transform social structures. In this sense events can be seen as actors that have important influences on social systems, particularly in linking localized small world networks with the global space of flows. These ideas are explored through the case of Barcelona, which illustrates the interplay between these different types of events in their total portfolio, and how the extension of ritual in the sense of Collins can also contribute to the generation of new relationships and practices in the contemporary network society. Barcelona is examined as an eventful city in which the alternation of continuity through iterative events and change through pulsar events contributes to increasing the network effects of events.

Keywords: Event effects; event portfolio; social practices; pulsar events; iterative events; Barcelona

1.5.3   Collaboration theory

Various forms of cooperation or partnership link stakeholders, but 'collaboration' goes beyond actions of mutual benefit. According to Gray (1989), collaboration is "a process of joint decision making among key stakeholders of a problem domain about the future of that domain" (Gray 1989:227). The 'domain' in question is variously an event, portfolios of events, the entire population of events in an area, or event-tourism at the destination level. The stakeholders are considered to be autonomous, but by engaging in joint decision-making they willingly give up a degree of independence – similar to the loss of complete independence when events become permanent institutions involving dependence on local government or other stakeholder support (Getz and Andersson, 2008).

Not all stakeholders will become partners or collaborators, but there are some common scenarios where it will be beneficial or necessary. Events that involve other organizations, as co-producers must establish a decision-making process that all can agree upon, and that is collaboration. Compromises might be necessary, and common goals agreed upon. Within cities or managed portfolios of events the actors, each an independent event organization plus agencies that co-ordinate and fund the collaborations, will want to share resources, marketing, office space, staff, venues, whatever. This cannot be done without a mechanism for joint decision-making. Within tourist destinations there might arise marketing consortia to promote event tourism that require more than each partner making a financial contribution; true collaboration will arise when these partners agree that a joint strategy and campaign works better than individual efforts, and all collaborators must agree on the terms and their responsibilities. In all cases, the collaborations involve more than co-operation, they bring people and organizations together in formal ways that create synergy.

Jamal and Getz (1995, p.190) laid out a process for collaboration among tourism partners that is applicable to many event management and tourism contexts. Step one is 'Problem-Setting', basically establishing the domain for collaboration – such as creating and managing an event portfolio among disparate partners. A number of facilitating conditions have to be discussed and established, namely:

♦   Recognition of interdependence (a precondition)
♦   Identification of the stakeholders (are they all at the table?)
♦   Perceptions of legitimacy among stakeholders (see the later discussion of legitimacy)
♦   Hire or co-opt a legitimate and skilled convener (this might be a first step)
♦   Positive beliefs about outcomes
♦   Balancing power among the collaborators
♦   A mandate for the collaboration
♦   Adequate resources to convene and enable collaboration

In the second step, 'Direction Setting', a shared vision and plan have to be worked out, preferably through consensus building. This might necessitate a lot of discussion about values and goals, resources and responsibilities. A critical decision-point will arise when it becomes clear that either consensus is possible or some other form of democratic voting will be required to move on. Failure will mean that true collaboration is not possible, at least among the assembled stakeholders. In the third and final step, 'Implementation', an action plan will be needed to ensure that tasks are completed. Monitoring and evaluation are required, plus ongoing efforts to ensure that the true spirit of collaboration is being pursued and not some hidden agenda by the more powerful. A question will always emerge – do we need a new organization to run the collaboration or can we all share in the administration?

The relevance of the 'political market square' is clear, and that concept is discussed later.

Research note

Jamal, T., & Getz, D. (1995) Collaboration theory and community tourism planning. *Annals of Tourism Research*, **22** (1), 186-204.

Abstract: This paper applies the theoretical constructs of collaboration to tourism destinations and offers insight into interorganizational collaboration for one specific tourism domain, the planning and development of local, community-based destinations. Drawing primarily from the literature on interorganizational relations, the theoretical constructs of collaboration are discussed. Challenges and considerations in the planning and development of local tourist destinations are then summarized followed by examples of community-based collaboration research. Propositions are presented for guiding collaborative initiatives and for investigating the application of collaboration theory to the planning and development of tourism destinations, from a community-involvement perspective.

Keywords: Collaboration, community-based tourism planning, stakeholders, propositions.

1.5.4 Social exchange theory

Why do people and organizations help each other? The nature of collaboration is that mutual benefits arise through synergies, with some loss of independence, and that suggests a rational process that can be called 'social exchange'. The Alonso and Bressan article (2013) examines stakeholder collaboration in light of social exchange theory.

Research note

Alonso, A. & Bressan, A. (2013) Stakeholders' perspectives on the evolution & benefits of a traditional wine festival: The case of the Grape Festival (*Festa dell'Uva*) in Impruneta, Italy. *Journal of Convention & Event Tourism*, **14**(4), 309-3.

Abstract: This study examines the perceived benefits of the *Festa dell'Uva* (Grape Festival) in Impruneta, mainly from local winery and other business owners. Overall, participants' comments identify the festival's significant shift of focus, which has resulted in a loss of its original purpose and undermined the wine sector's importance. The findings align with some of the tenets of social exchange theory, and have important implications for the future of wine and food festivals. For instance, at times when many communities face socio-economic challenges, preserving their traditional food culture can be vital to maintain their identity.

Keywords: Food and wine festivals, stakeholders, social exchange theory, perceptions, Impruneta

Discussion questions

1   Discuss the difference between a stakeholder and a shareholder.

2   Why is it important to understand who is our internal and external stakeholders?

3   What is the role of stakeholder theory to event management and tourism?

4   Discuss social responsibility and how it influences stakeholder management.

5   Understand the relevance of systems theory, social network theory, collaboration theory and social exchange theory.

Assessment activities

Visit one of the major planned events in your area and identify its internal and external stakeholders. Try to understand which theories can be used to explain the stakeholders' interactions and how to manage them.

Recommended additional readings and resources

Chappelet, J-L., & Parent, M. (eds.) (2015). *Routledge Handbook of Sports Event Management*. London: Routledge.

References

Alonso, A. & Bressan, A. (2013) Stakeholders' perspectives on the evolution and benefits of a traditional wine festival: The case of the Grape Festival ("Festa dell'Uva") in Impruneta, Italy. *Journal of Convention & Event Tourism*, **14** (4), 309-3.

Andersson, T. D., & Getz, D. (2009). Tourism as a mixed industry: Differences between private, public and not-for-profit festivals. *Tourism Management*, 30(6), 847-856.

Anuar, A. N. A., Ahmed, H., Jusoh, H., & Hussain, M. Y. (2012). Understanding the role of stakeholder in the formation of tourist friendly destination concept. *Journal of Management & Sustainability*, **2**, 69.

Booth, A. (2016). Negotiating diasporic culture: Festival collaborations and production networks. *International Journal of Event and Festival Management*, **7** (2), 100 - 116.

Byrd, E. (2007). Stakeholders in sustainable tourism development and their roles: Applying stakeholder theory to sustainable tourism development. *Tourism Review*, **62** (2), 6-13.

Castells, M. (2009), *The Rise of the Network Society: The Information Age*, 2nd ed., Wiley-Blackwell, Hoboken, NJ.

Castells, M. (2011). A network theory of power. *International Journal of Communication*, **5** (15), 773-787.

Carroll, A.B. (1993). *Business and Society: Ethics and Stakeholder Management*, 2nd Edn. Cincinnati: South-Western.

Chacko, H. E., & Schaffer, J. D. (1993). The evolution of a festival: Creole Christmas in New Orleans. *Tourism Management*, **14**(6), 475-482.

Chappelet, J. L., & Parent, M. M. (2015). The (wide) world of sports events. In Chappelet, J-L., & Parent, M. (eds.) *Routledge Handbook of Sports Event Management*, 1-17. London: Routledge.

Colbry, S., Hurwitz, M., Adair, R. (2014) Collaboration Theory. *Journal Of Leadership Education*, **13**(4), 63-75.

d'Angella, F., & Go, F. M. (2009). Tale of two cities' collaborative tourism marketing: Towards a theory of destination stakeholder assessment. *Tourism Management*, **30**(3), 429-440

Freeman, R.E. (1984). *Strategic Management: A Stakeholder Approach*. Boston: Pitman.

Freeman, R.E (2004). A stakeholder theory of modern corporations. In Beauchamp, T.L. & Bowie, N.E. (eds.) *Ethical Theory and Business*, Prentice Hall, Upper Saddle River, pp.56-65.

Frisby, W., & Getz, D. (1989). Festival management: A case study perspective. *Journal of Travel Research*, **28**(1), 7-11.

Garrod, B., Fyall, A., Leask, A., & Reid, E. (2012). Engaging residents as stakeholders of the visitor attraction. *Tourism Management*, **33** (5), 1159-1173.

Getz, D. & Andersson, T. (2008). Sustainable festivals: On becoming an institution. *Event Management*, **12**, 1-17.

Getz, D., T. Andersson, & M. Larson (2007). Festival stakeholder roles: Concepts and case studies. *Event Management*, **10** (2/3), 103-122.

Getz, D., & Frisby, W. (1988). Evaluating management effectiveness in community-run festivals. *Journal of Travel Research*, **27**(1), 22-27.

Getz, D. & Jamal, T. (1994). The environment-community symbiosis: A case for collaborative tourism planning. *Journal of Sustainable Tourism*, **2** (3), 152-173.

Getz, D., & Page, S. (2016). *Event Studies: Theory, Research and Policy for Planned Events*, 3rd ed. Routledge.

Gray, B. (1989). Collaborating: Finding Common Ground for Multiparty Problems. San Francisco: Jossey-Bass.

Hannah, L., Midgley, G., Andelman, S., Araújo, M., Hughes, G., Martinez-Meyer, E., ... & Williams, P. (2007). Protected area needs in a changing climate. *Frontiers in Ecology and the Environment*, **5**(3), 131-138

Heenan, D. A. (1978). Tourism and the community a drama in three acts. *Journal of Travel Research*, **16**(4), 30-32.

Investopedia, LLC. (2018). Shareholder. Retrieved from https://www.investopedia.com/terms/s/shareholder.asp

Izzo, F., Bonetti, E., & Masiello, B. (2012). Strong ties within cultural organization event networks and local development in a tale of three festivals. *Event Management*, **16**, 223–244.

Jamal, T. B., & Getz, D. (1995). Collaboration theory and community tourism planning. *Annals of Tourism Research*, **22** (1), 186-204.

Jarman, D., Theodoraki, E., Hall, H., & Ali-Knight, J. (2014). Social network analysis and festival cities: An exploration of concepts, literature and methods. *International Journal of Event and Festival Management*, **5** (3), 311-322.

Karlsen, S., & Stenbacka Nordström, C. (2009). Festivals in the Barents region: exploring festival-stakeholder cooperation. *Scandinavian Journal of Hospitality and Tourism*, **9**(2-3), 130-145.

Larson, M. (2002). A political approach to relationship marketing: Case study of the Storsjöyran Festival. *International Journal of Tourism Research*, **4**(2), 119-143.

Larson, M. (2009). Joint event production in the jungle, the park, and the garden: Metaphors of event networks. *Tourism Management*, **30**(3), 393-399.

Larson, M., & Wikström, E. (2001). Organizing events: Managing conflict and consensus in a political market square. *Event Management*, **7**(1), 51-65.

Lewis, J. (2018). Central hub for concert weekend. Retrieved from: https://www.odt.co.nz/news/dunedin/central-hub-concert-weekend

Musgrave, J., & Woodward, S. (2016). Ecological systems theory approach to corporate social responsibility: Contextual perspectives from meeting planners. *Event Management*, **20**, 365–381.

Reid, S., & Arcodia, C. (2002). Understanding the role of the stakeholder in event management.Paper presented at the Events and Placemaking Conference, Sydney, Australia.

Richards, G. (2015). Events in the network society: The role of pulsar and iterative events. *Event Management*, **19**, 553–566.

Savage, G., Nix, T., Whitehead, C., & Blair, J. (1991). Strategies for assessing and managing organizational stakeholders. *Academy of Management Executives*, **5** (2), 61-75.

Sheehan, L., & Ritchie, J. R. B. (2005). Destination stakeholders: Exploring identity and salience. *Annals of Tourism Research*, **32** (3), 711-734.

Van Niekerk, M. (2014). The role of the public sector in tourism destination management from a network relationship approach. *Tourism Analysis*, **19**, 701–718.

Van Niekerk, M. (2016). The applicability and usefulness of the stakeholder strategy matrix for festival management. *Event Management*, **20**, 165-179.

WebFinance Inc. (2018). Stakeholder Theory. Retrieved from http://www.businessdictionary.com/definition/stakeholder-theory.html

Wikipedia. (2018a). System Theory. Retrieved from https://en.wikipedia.org/wiki/Systems_theory

Wikipedia. (2018b). Social Network Theory. Retrieved from https://en.wikipedia.org/wiki/Social_network

Wikipedia. (2018c). Social Exchange Theory. Retrieved from https://en.wikipedia.org/wiki/Social_exchange_theory

Wood, E. H. (2006). Measuring the social impacts of local authority events: A pilot study for a civic pride scale. *International Journal of Nonprofit and Voluntary Sector Marketing*, **11**(3), 165-179.

Yukl, G., Chavez, C., & Seifert, C. F. (2005). Assessing the construct validity and utility of two new influence tactics. *Journal of Organizational Behavior*, **26**, 705- 725.

Ziakas, V., and Costa, C. (2010). Explicating inter-organizational linkages of a host community's events network. *International Journal of Event and Festival Management*, **1** (2), 132-147.

2 Perspectives on Stakeholder Theory

Learning objectives

At the end of the chapter readers should be able to:

☐ Differentiate between the descriptive/empirical, instrumental, managerial, and normative perspectives on stakeholder theory

☐ Understand the Clarkson Principles in the context of Corporate Social Responsibility (CSR)

☐ Describe Carroll's CSR Pyramid Model adapted and modified for events and tourism

☐ Identify primary and secondary stakeholders; active and passive

☐ Define and classify stakeholders

☐ Demonstrate stakeholder salience (combining power, legitimacy, and urgency) in the context of events and tourism

☐ Compare event and tourism stakeholders and their roles

2.1 Introduction

This chapter provides elaboration of stakeholder theory, commencing with four general perspectives on stakeholder theory as identified by Donaldson and Preston (1995). This is followed by a discussion of how CSR or corporate social responsibility has influenced thinking about stakeholders and forms an integral part of the normative perspective. Carroll's (1993) popular CSR model has been adapted and modified for this book, providing a more integrated and relevant approach.

Defining and classifying stakeholders is the third major topic covered, drawing first on generic stakeholder theory and commencing with a discussion of primary and secondary, active and passive stakeholders. Particularly attention is given to the framework provided by Mitchell, Agle and Wood (1997) that defines 'stockholder salience' as a combination of 'legitimacy, power and urgency'. These terms are explored in detail. The chapter concludes with an examination of event and tourism stakeholders, including a diagram and research notes from the events and tourism literature.

2.2 Key terms defined

Primary stakeholders

Primary stakeholders are those stakeholders that have a direct stake in the organization and its success. (Clarkson, 1995).

Secondary stakeholders

Secondary stakeholders are those that have a public or special interest stake in the organization. (Clarkson, 1995).

Active stakeholders

Active stakeholders want to be involved and therefore require a variety of engagement efforts, from public meetings to inclusion on boards of directors. (Ponsford and Williams, 2010).

Passive stakeholders

Passive stakeholders just want to be kept informed, necessitating attention to the various media that can best reach them, and to two-way communication channels. (Ponsford and Williams, 2010).

2.3 Case study - Commonwealth Games, Gold Coast Australia

Karin Weber – Hong Kong Polytechnic University – Hong Kong

Xin Jin – Griffith University - Australia

Overview of the Games

The Commonwealth Games are an international sport event involving athletes from the Commonwealth of Nations. Similar to the Olympic Games, the event is held every four years. The Games have taken place since 1930, only interrupted twice by the Second World War in 1942 and 1946. The event evolved with the decolonisation of the British Empire, reflected in the title change of the event from British Empire Games (1930-1950) to the British Empire and Commonwealth Games (1970-1974) and finally, the Commonwealth Games since 1978. Rituals and symbols, such as the Games flag and Queen's Baton, as well as opening and closing ceremonies still carry a legacy, tradition, and British effect. Only six nations have attended every Commonwealth Games: Australia, Canada, England, New Zealand, Scotland, and Wales. Only three games were hosted outside of these six nations, twice in Asia (Malaysia and India) and once in the Caribbean (Jamaica). The Commonwealth Games are overseen by the Commonwealth Games Federation (CGF) which also controls the sporting program and selects the host cities. The games movement consists of the International

Sports Federations, Commonwealth Games Associations and organising committees for each Commonwealth Games. Apart from many Olympic sports, the Games also include some sports that are played predominantly in Commonwealth countries but which are not part of the Olympic program, such as lawn bowls, netball, and squash. A survey by the authors indicated that games and medals, Commonwealth of Nations, star athletes, the opening and closing ceremonies, and the host cities are the top associations related to the event.

GC2018

The Gold Coast 2018 Commonwealth Games were hosted at the Gold Coast, Australia from 4-15 April 2018. They were managed by the Gold Coast 2018 Commonwealth Games Corporation (GOLDOC), formed by the Government of Queensland. GOLDOC, a statutory body, having one chairman and 12 Board members, was responsible to the Minister for the Commonwealth Games. There were eight divisions within the organisation that respectively were responsible for executive, commercial, communications and marketing, strategic engagement, finance and business services, sport and operations, venues and services, and planning and readiness. GC2018 Games partners also included the City of Gold Coast, Commonwealth Games Australia, and Office of the Commonwealth Games. GC2018 was the world's first multi-sport event which inaugurated an equal number of women's and men's medal events. It was also a multi-sport event that included athletes with a disability as full members of their national teams, ensuring that their medals were included in the medal count.

Photo 2.1: Official mascot . Picture credit: Author's own K. Weber.

The main venue for GC2018 was Carrara Stadium, which hosted the opening and closing ceremony; its seating capacity was increased to 40,000 during the Games by the installation of a large temporary North Stand. About 16 other venues at the Gold Coast, in Brisbane, Cairns and Townsville hosted the competitions or the preliminary rounds of basketball competitions. More than 4,000 athletes from 71 Commonwealth Games Associations participated in the Games, watched by an estimated 16 million viewers in Australia, and 1.5 billion viewers worldwide. During the Games, the GC2018 website attracted around 113 million (69 million unique) page views, while the various social media channels had around 733,600 followers and more than 108.3 million impressions.

The Queensland state government spent about A$1.5 billion for the delivery of the event, mainly on venues and the Games Village, the procurement program, and security. A pre-game economic impact study indicated that expenditures from both government and private sectors on infrastructure construction was the main contributing factor to pre-games economic impacts. Key sources of direct revenue for the Games included broadcast rights, sponsorship, ticket sales, licensing, visitor expenditures, interest, and related services. Broadcast rights were estimated to be a key revenue source, despite large markets (such as China and the USA) potentially not being covered for TV broadcast (as they were not participating in the Commonwealth Games). Apart from attracting visitors during the game year, the event was estimated to attract induced visitors during post-game years due to enhanced destination awareness. Induced tourism effects to the host city could also spill over to other states in Australia, with the event and its advertising campaigns also potentially acting as a catalyst for promoting exports for other major Queensland industries (for example, food products, education, professional services, health and entertainment). It was estimated that the Games would generate about 16,000 jobs on an FTE basis (Jones, 2018; Pham et al. 2018).

Community

With the aim of leading the local community to a healthier, active and sustainable lifestyle, as well as using the event as a way to promote community pride, GOLDOC and the local city council developed a series of Connect Community programs. These programs sought to engage community groups from across the state, and involve them in the delivery and sharing of game experiences. Organisers developed the Reconciliation Action Plan, which aimed to engage and strengthen respect between Aboriginal and Torres Strait Islanders and other Australians. They also developed the Festival 2018 program on the Gold Coast – cultural programs that engaged the local community during the event. The community legacy programs not only targeted residents of the host sites but all Queensland residents as to instil an increased sense of community. Education programs and related cultural programs were rolled out across Queensland's schools as a legacy for community engagement. Cultural activities engaged local residents and visitors in the lead-up to, during and after GC2018. However, anecdotal evidence also indicated that culturally and linguistically distinct communities were less engaged due to social and cultural reasons. GC2108 has been very successful in volunteer participation – an indicator of community engagement - with 15,000 volunteers, called 'game shapers', invigorating this event with their high spirit and services.

Disputes indicating stakeholder conflicts

The opening and closing ceremony were designed and run by a US event company, alongside with GOLDOC. Despite this US event company's prior experience of staging numerous large scale sporting events, GC2018 closing ceremony was highly criticized for not showing the athletes (including the flagbearer) entering the stadium in the TV broadcast. The level of uproar on social media resulted in an apology from the GOLDOC chairman. There were also disputes between the TV channel which won the broadcast rights and the actual host broadcasters (the event organizer) as to who was to blame, whether the broadcaster was briefed on athletes not to be featured, and whether the TV channel could start the broadcast 15 minutes earlier to capture the arrival of the athletes. The event organizer was also described by a TV host as an "arty farty entertainment organizer" who "doesn't know what the Games are all about". In addition, the closing ceremony was criticized for its formalities and performing pro-grams. The fact that a large number of athletes left the ceremony early indicated that it did not achieve its aim of celebrating athletes' accomplishment and providing them with a great final experience.

In an effort to manage traffic, the event organizers launched a campaign for locals and spectators to stay off the highway that connects the Gold Coast and Brisbane, and use public transportation instead. However, the campaign became a 'scare cam-paign,' resulting in the highway being unusually empty during the Games, and locals fleeing from the city to have family holidays elsewhere to avoid road closures and other inconveniences. Local businesses complained that this scare tactic resulted in a significant drop in revenue in certain parts of the city. GOLDOC, the State Govern-ment, the local city council and tourism bodies were all criticized by local businesses. The Games organizer admitted that they scared people off with fears of traffic chaos, although they took action and lured people back to share the event experience. Anecdotal evidence and interviews by reporters and academic research supported the crowd-off effect, but statistics are lacking to assess the loss of revenue to local restaurants and the reduction in occupancy rates of local hotels. Game visitors were also different from leisure tourists in terms of expenditure and shopping behaviors which could have contributed to the perception of low business for local restaurants. Many GC2018 visitors also choose to stay in Airbnb accommodation instead of hotels and serviced apartments. The crowd-off effect may also have resulted in bringing eco-nomic benefits to family holiday destinations in Australia, New Zealand or other short-haul local or international destinations. Thus, the allocation of economic benefits to businesses and revenue leakages of GC2018 could be different from those of previous multi-sport events.

As is apparent from this case, while the GC2018 were largely considered a success with numerous benefits for the wider community, there was also considerable scope for improvement of stakeholder engagement/relations.

2.4   Four perspectives on stakeholder theory

As mentioned, 'stakeholder theory' is not a unified, coherent model or set of principles. In fact, there are four perspectives or 'theses' to be considered, and they are all relevant to events and tourism management.

2.4.1 Descriptive/empirical

A basic tenet in the Donaldson and Preston perspective is that corporations exist as collections of both collaborative and competitive interests. Researchers study how organizations work in this environment and what happens in the real world. Researchers (or managers) identify and analyze the stakeholders of an organization and how the relationships are managed, as well as how this affects the organization. Owners/managers can be asked to do a stakeholder map (explained later) as a tool in exploring relationships. This was the approach taken by Getz et al. (2007) in describing the often overlapping and dynamic roles of festival stakeholders. Description is often the first step in theory development, and this kind of knowledge can help managers in a value-free manner.

2.4.2 Instrumental

This approach requires determination of how stakeholder relationships and their management actually affect the organization and achievement of its goals. Ideally, propositions follow on how to manage stakeholders for optimum results.

A key question for events is this: what strategies work best to obtain permanent support from key stakeholders such as local authorities? Theory derived from this approach can be used to provide guidance to managers. For example, it is quite clear from a wide range of research that ignoring certain external stakeholders is likely to lead to serious problems for organizations. Event researchers have also identified the advantages of forging long-term sponsorship relationships, and of inviting key stakeholders to join the decision-making process; it has also been found that festival managers often pursue a strategy of institutionalization, that is ensuring permanent support from vital stakeholder in exchange for giving up some degree of independence (Getz and Andersson, 2008).

While this perspective is crucial in theory development, it does not result in predictive capabilities. For example, knowing that many festival managers pursue a strategy of institutionalization does not suggest that all should do it, or that it is feasible, but it gives a strong indication of how certain strategies might work in different situations.

2.4.3 Managerial

Ideally, research and analysis should lead to theory with general applicability across most or all situations. This theory might consist of managerial guidelines, recommended practices, structures, and attitudes to be adopted by managers. This is different from a normative approach based on philosophy or ideology.

2.4.4 Normative

In the normative perspective (i.e., a value-based approach), stakeholders are believed to have legitimate interests in the focal organization, meaning that their interests are of intrinsic value to the organization. Donaldson and Preston believed that corporations have moral or ethical obligations to take into account the stakeholders who can affect, or are affected by its actions. This links directly with corporate social responsibility and the notion of a *social license to operate* (discussed later).

Many festivals and events in the public and not-for-profit sectors will subscribe to a normative approach, believing that they have an obligation to consult and engage their most salient stakeholders – especially the public at large. Because of widespread demands for sustainable development and accountability, in many jurisdictions events are being required to adopt new policies and practices that reflect responsibility and sustainability principles.

When 'gurus' give advice, managers have to ask "where does this come from?" Is it based solely on philosophy or ideology, or is there a foundation of research and theory behind it? Concepts like CSR have gained widespread acceptance for moral reasons, but there is also some weight of research backing it. The evidence suggests that corporations might be more successful when they behave in an ethical manner and consider the needs of their stakeholders. For government agencies and charitable organizations this principle should be taken for granted.

2.4.5 The Clarkson Principles of stakeholder management

In the normative approach the Clarkson Principles of Stakeholder Management are often cited (Caux Round Table for Moral Capitalism, 2018). We can call these 'tenets' (i.e., principles or beliefs) and find them to be of particular relevance to events in the public and not-for-profit domains, as those events are almost always devoted to public service. Their applicability to private, for-profit events will depend in part on the philosophy of owners and managers, and on the pressures placed on them by their stakeholders. DMOs or development corporations with narrow mandates might be tempted to ignore these principles, but that strategy is likely to lead to serious difficulties.

Below you can find The Clarkson Principles of Stakeholder Management (Caux Round Table for Moral Capitalism, 2018) and some comments that have been added by the authors, indicated in italics:

1   Managers should acknowledge and actively monitor the concerns of all legitimate stakeholders, and should take their interests appropriately into account in decision-making and operations.

      'Legitimacy' is fully explained later. To 'monitor' concerns will require a permanent mechanism for stakeholder input.

2   Managers should listen to and openly communicate with stakeholders about their respective concerns and contributions, and about the risks that they assume because of their involvement with the corporation.

Risks *are a key concern. For example, suppliers take financial risks (will they get paid?) and partners or co-producers share liabilities if something goes wrong.*

3   Managers should adopt processes and modes of behavior that are sensitive to the concerns and capabilities of each stakeholder constituency.

'Constituency' can be a synonym for stakeholder group; events and tourism organizations typically have these major constituencies: the community (residents); members, or the industry; local government and politicians, and the media. Customers or target market segments are also critical constituencies.

4   Managers should recognize the interdependence of efforts and rewards among stakeholders, and should attempt to achieve a fair distribution of the benefits and burdens of corporate activity among them, taking into account their respective risks and vulnerabilities.

'Interdependencies' among stakeholders requires careful analysis, and that is part of stakeholder mapping. Power relations have to be considered (see the 'political market square'). The notion of 'fairness' is a tricky one, and likely to generate lots of discussion about the distribution of costs, benefits and risks.

5   Managers should work cooperatively with other entities; both public and private, to insure that risks and harms arising from corporate activities are minimized and, where they cannot be avoided, appropriately compensated.

'Work cooperatively' leads to the concept of collaboration theory. Basically, evidence shows that working together is often a better strategy than competition, especially in the not-for-profit sector.

6   Managers should avoid altogether activities that might jeopardize inalienable human rights (e.g., the right to life) or give rise to risks, which, if clearly understood, would be patently unacceptable to relevant stakeholders.

This principle is usually reinforced by laws and regulations. Event organizers should be familiar with the laws and by-laws of the countries and cities that they operate in. This will ensure compliance with the necessary regulations.

7   Managers should acknowledge the potential conflicts between (a) their own role as corporate stakeholders, and (b) their legal and moral responsibilities for the interests of stakeholders, and should address such conflicts through open communication, appropriate reporting and incentive systems and, where necessary, third party review.

'Agency theory' is alluded to in this principle, referencing the 'principle-agent' issue that arises when managers (or other agents representing someone-else's interests) fail in their fiduciary responsibility and act in their own interest. Managers in the public and not-for-profit event sectors might be conflicted

in deciding between their duty to politicians or directors and their perceived
responsibility to other stakeholders, including the public at large. Here, the
ethics of professionalism enter the picture in a big way. Outside audits and
reviews might be needed to sort out such issues. How open and accountable is
the organization?

2.5 Social responsibility for events and tourism

A popular model by Carroll (1993) provides a foundation for considering social
responsibility within a wider sustainability paradigm. The pyramid-shaped
model (easily found online) displays on one side the responsibilities of a firm,
starting with economics at the base (surviving, making a profit, generating a
return on investment), then legal, ethical and finally philanthropic responsibilities at the peak. On the other side are guiding principles, with "be a good
corporate citizen" at the apex. Applying this normative approach to events will
depend on their orientation, service versus/plus profit, and their roles in various government or corporate policies and strategies. For a nonprofit devoted to
community service it might be appropriate to turn the pyramid upside down,
although that raises the necessity of staying financially viable (now at the peak
instead of the base) in order to meet philanthropic or social goals and that could
be a risky strategy. We have modified the Carroll model (see Figure 2.1) to reflect
a sustainability paradigm.

Figure 2.1: An integrated model of social responsibility for events and tourism. Source:
Adapted from Carroll (1993)

In this revision all four types of responsibility are of equal importance, and integrated within a planning and evaluation framework. Regarding stakeholders, the implications are many. Within the economic domain the necessity for financial viability remains, but the mandate or responsibility is extended to creating economic prosperity for all (being the community or nation). This challenges the typical mandate of member-based DMOs - which is to support member interests - and suggests the responsibility of events and tourism is much wider. Public-private partnerships are more likely to adopt this orientation.

The philanthropic domain stresses support for charities and the host community, something that many events and tourism organizations incorporate in their mandate. This CSR role can also include education on important issues, or even social marketing to foster worthwhile causes. In the legal domain are all the rules and regulations that must be obeyed, but within the CSR and sustainability paradigms applying to stakeholder management, why not go beyond the basics and become leaders? Fourthly, the ethical domain pertains to professionalism, and in the context of normative stakeholder theory the notion of treating all legitimate stakeholders fairly. This latter point requires thinking about what defines legitimacy, as discussed later. Sustainability policies have been added to the ethical domain, because they are not found in all legal systems or political environments.

Research notes

These papers explain 'social license to operate' within the contexts of social responsibility and stakeholder theory.

Ponsford, I. & Williams, P. (2010). Crafting a social license to operate: a case study of Vancouver 2010's Cypress Olympic venue. *Event Management*, **14** (1), 17-36.

Abstract: Olympic Games often require organizing committees to construct major sports venues. As private entities not clearly accountable to the public, these organizing committees or 'Olympic Corporations' have been accused of bypassing normal planning protocols, and in the process transforming the nature of host cities with little stakeholder consultation. This article traces the evolution of relationships between Vancouver 2010's Olympic Corporation and stakeholders concerned with Cypress Olympic Venue (COV) development. It suggests that because a balance of power existed between the Olympic Corporation and stakeholder groups, the relationship transformed from being primarily antagonistic to a more constructive configuration through successive interactions. While the Olympic Corporation's stakeholder engagement strategies appear successful at the COV, stakeholder respondents still exhibit skepticism about Olympic organizers. This article emphasizes the importance of crafting a 'social license to operate' in the Olympic planning context and uncovers some essential prerequisites for the development of corporate-community relationships.

Keywords: corporate social responsibility; Olympic Games; social license to operate; stakeholder engagement; sustainability; Vancouver 2010

Williams, P., Gill, A., Marcoux, J., & Xu, N. (2012). Nurturing 'social license to operate' through corporate-civil relationships in tourism destinations. In C. Hsu and W. Gartner (eds.), *The Routledge Handbook of Tourism Research*, pp. 196-214. London: Routledge.

These authors discuss the corporate-community stakeholder framework, with explicit reference to stakeholder theory, in the context of social responsibility and social license to operate. The setting is the resort of Whistler, British Columbia, a host for many events including the 2010 Winter Olympics.

2.6 Typology and classification of stakeholders

Organizations must consider the interests of both internal and external stakeholders, and these relationships have to be managed. Some relationships are more important than others giving rise to a common distinction between 'primary' and 'secondary' stakeholders as described by Clarkson (1995), or Ponsford and Williams (2010), who took a slightly different perspective, distinguishing between 'active' and 'passive' stakeholders.

These terms are open to interpretation and their applicability has to consider the circumstances of the organization and its external relationships. They were both previously discussed in the chapter. Just who is a stakeholder is open to judgment. Do they include competitor events? Does it incorporate the public at large? Are environmental lobby groups included?

Perhaps a better approach than sorting stakeholders into rather ambiguous primary and secondary categories is that recommended by Mitchell et al. (1997). They argued that stakeholders could be classified according to three attributes that, taken together, determine the salience of stakeholders (each of these is later examined in detail):

♦ **Power:** can they impose their will and directly threaten or influence your organization? This category typically includes regulators and funders.

♦ **Legitimacy:** The organizers can attempt to determine who has a legitimate claim to be heard, but political reality and social responsibility might widen the scope of legitimacy; others can make a claim that has to be evaluated. Community festivals are likely to have a much wider definition of legitimate stakeholders than corporate meetings and association conferences.

♦ **Urgency:** how urgent is a stakeholder's demands or claims? Usually regulators have to be satisfied right away (e.g., fire, police, health and safety). Some lobby groups might take a long-term perspective on events in general, reflecting their social and environmental concerns.

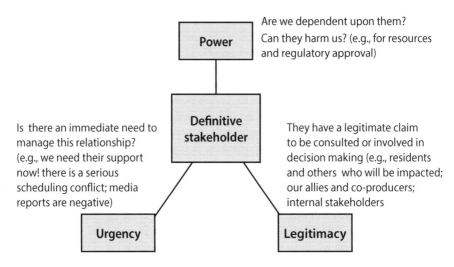

Figure 2.2: Stakeholder typology: one, two or three attributes present. Source: Adapted from Mitchell et al. (1997)

When all three attributes of salience are combined, the stakeholders were called 'definitive' by Mitchell et al. (1997).There remains an open question: is there such a thing as a 'non-stakeholder'? Probably it is wiser to think in terms of 'dormant stakeholders' who are not currently of interest, but might become important. Appropriate strategies for each of the categories in this diagram are discussed later.

2.6.1 Power

Power is commonly defined as the ability to act in a particular way (such as to create an event) or to influence others (possibly, but not necessarily against their will or preferences). It is a concept closely related to legitimacy, and power sometimes derives from the same sources, particularly law, control of information and resources. Power can be used for good or bad, and as such is open to interpretation. A starting point is the work of the philosopher Foucault (1926-1984) who equated control of knowledge with power. In Foucault's conceptualization those who control information or determine what is considered within any discourse (e.g., what are the topics of importance in event studies?) hold power (The Stanford Encyclopedia of Philosophy, 2016). Foucault argued that power is omnipresent at every level of the social body, and so we should always be looking at relationships with the idea that power is being used by someone or group for some purpose. Foucault identified '*sovereign power*' which involves obedience to the law, and in the events realm this involves numerous laws and regulations that must be obeyed. '*Pastoral power*' was identified as the convergence of techniques, rationalities and practices designed to govern or guide people's conduct, and this can include social norms and political correctness.

Knowledge is connected to power, and we can see in contemporary society how large corporations use data for their commercial purposes, and governments do the same for security. Data hacks have become so common that it proves the point that knowledge is power.

Mitchell, Agle, and Wood (1997) said there are three types of power that are highly relevant to stakeholder theory:

- **Coercive power**: based on physical resources of force, violence, or restraint
- **Utilitarian power**: based on financial or material resources
- **Normative power**: based on symbolic resources such as being able to command attention of the media

It is always important to examine who has power, what kinds they wield, and how it is used. Looking back to Figure 2.2, each category of stakeholder might possess different types of power applied to tourism and events. Power is an enduring topic of interest to event scholars, and it usually links directly to stakeholder management issues. In the three ensuing research notes, first Jepson et al. (2014) discuss power in the context of inclusive community engagement in festivals. Andersson and Getz (2007) look at the relative bargaining power of stakeholders, with implications for financial viability. Tiew et al. (2015) link power to the saliency of stakeholders and find that those with resources have the most power.

Research notes

Jepson, A., Clarke, A. & Ragsdell, G. (2014). Investigating the application of the motivation–opportunity–ability model to reveal factors, which facilitate or inhibit inclusive engagement within local community festivals. *Scandinavian Journal of Hospitality and Tourism*, **14** (3), 331-348.

Abstract: Currently there is limited understanding, agreement, and research within the phenomena of community engagement and participation in local community festivals and events. This article aims to contribute to this growing, but limited, debate by justifying the adaption and integration of the Motivation – Opportunity – Ability (MOA) model, and proposing a combination of primary data collection and analysis methods, to reveal and understand the factors that either inhibit or facilitate local community engagement in festivals and events. The rationale of this conceptual article is to determine how sustainability can be defined and achieved within local community festivals and events, by developing sustainable and inclusive community networks where the local population is actively engaged within the creation of events.

The article begins by exploring the literature surrounding communities, community festivals and events, and community engagement. The article then moves on to discuss the MOA model and its adaption and application to event studies.

It builds on concepts discussed by Jepson, Clarke, and Ragsdell (2012) that support the creation of inclusive community festivals and events through inclusive participation within the planning and decision-making process. The article then moves on to explore the methodological concerns triggered by this model, such as the need to be adaptable and flexible across a multifaceted community event with regard to collecting primary data whilst maintaining integrity and validity during analysis. Finally, the article comments on the overall suitability of the MOA model to capture primary data and draw conclusions about best practice for community engagement in local festivals and events.

Keywords: engagement, inclusion, community festivals, MOA model, event planning

Andersson, T. & Getz, D. (2007). Resource dependency, costs and revenues of a street festival. *Tourism Economics*, **13** (1), 143-162.

Abstract: The financial position of a tourism-oriented street festival in Sweden is examined within the context of resource dependency and stakeholder management theory, focused on testing two hypotheses derived from this theoretical base. Data from a five-year period revealed how costs associated with the strongest stakeholders (that is, with the greatest bargaining power) greatly increased relative to costs associated with weak stakeholders. The festival was also more able to increase its revenues from weak stakeholders than from those in strong bargaining positions. Conclusions are drawn on how this case confirms and elaborates upon theory, particularly by applying it to the festival sector. Management implications are also drawn on how festival organizations should manage relationships when they hold strong or weak positions relative to stakeholders.

Keywords: festival costs and revenues; resource dependency; stakeholder management

Tiew, F., Holmes, K., & De Bussy, N. (2015). Tourism events and the nature of stakeholder power. *Event Management*, **19**, 525-541.

Abstract: This exploratory case study examines the power relations among the stakeholders of a tourism event in Borneo. It examines the sources of stakeholder power and the pattern of interdependence of various stakeholders, primarily based on interviews with event managers and stakeholders, as well as field visits. An analysis of the different types and amount of resource control, dependency, and network centrality resulted in four different categories of stakeholder power patterns—executive, asset based, referral, and diffuse stakeholders. The study also found that resource-based power was the primary source of power, whereas network-based power was a secondary and supplementary source. The case study revealed that the salience of event stakeholders based on their power was highly variable due to the different types of power that they had. This article contributes to the literature of event tourism, a typology of the event stakeholder

powers in a predominately government-owned music festival, and offered practical suggestions to event management. It also advances the stakeholder power
concept within event tourism studies.

Keywords: Tourism event; stakeholder power; resource dependency; network
centrality; stakeholder salience

2.6.2 Urgency

In daily life we can understand urgency in terms of need (e.g., biological or
financial) or pressing requirements (e.g., the demands of a boss) to take immediate action. Urgency might be self-perceived and internalized, or arise from
the demands or persistence of someone else, such as a powerful stakeholder. If
actions can easily or without cost be deferred or ignored, there is little urgency,
but of course this depends on an assessment of the risk entailed, or of penalties
that might be imposed. Events are often very time-sensitive when it comes to
financial health, with expenditures generally preceding revenue. Accordingly,
if a creditor demands immediate re-payment, prior to ticket sales, all could be
lost. On the other hand, if sponsors can be convinced to give money up front,
the event managers might very well provide special considerations because they
have an urgent need for cash.

In tourism, urgency can often be witnessed when disaster strikes and an
immediate response is required to restore confidence or counter negative publicity. Also, a failure of one market segment to generate expected demand, such as
a sudden decline in conference bookings, can require an urgent response from
DMOs and event venues. Because tourism is almost universal in scope and enormous in scale, in many cities, resorts and regions it is only the sudden absence or
threat of boycott that sparks calls for urgent action. Changes in tourism-related
forces and trends can be incremental and barely noticeable, giving rise to com-
placency, and in the events sector this can happen in well-established events that
fail to monitor and adapt.

Parent and Deephouse (2007) doing research in the sports event sector examined how stakeholders were prioritized based on their perceived power, urgency
and legitimacy.

Research note

Parent, M. M. & Deephouse, D. L. (2007). A case study of stakeholder identifi-
    cation and prioritization by managers. *Journal of Business Ethics*, 75(1), 1-23.

Abstract: The purpose of this article is to examine stakeholder identification and
prioritization by managers using the power, legitimacy, and urgency framework of Mitchell et al. (1997). We use a multi-method, comparative case study
of two large-scale sporting event-organizing committees, with a particular focus

on interviews with managers at three hierarchical levels. We support the positive relationship between number of stakeholder attributes and perceived stakeholder salience. Managers' hierarchical level and role have direct and moderating effects on stakeholder identification and perceived salience. We also found that most stakeholders were definitive, dominant, or dormant types – the other five types were rare. Power has the most important effect on salience, followed by urgency and legitimacy. Based on our case study, we offer several ways to advance the theory of stakeholder identification and salience.

Keywords: case study, interview, data, relationship, stakeholder, stakeholder management, stakeholder theory

2.6.3 Legitimacy

Suchman (1995) defined legitimacy as "a generalized perception or assumption that the actions of an entity are desirable, proper, appropriate within some socially constructed system of norms, values, beliefs, and definitions" (p. 574). *Pragmatic legitimacy*, as Suchman defined it, can be interpreted as public or stakeholder acceptance of a tourism organization or event, weighing perceived costs and benefits from a self-interest point of view. *Moral legitimacy* relates to perceptions of legal and ethical behavior. When society or stakeholders accept that an organization or event is necessary and/or inevitable, it holds *cognitive legitimacy*.

Who can make a legitimate claim to being consulted or involved in decision-making? For example, can environmental lobby groups assume that an event must include them in their planning and impact assessments, or is it up to the event owners and managers to decide who should be included, consulted, or ignored based on a rational evaluation of salience? Parsons (1960) argued that organizations that pursue goals in line with social values have a legitimate claim on resources, and this is the 'public good' claim put forward by many festivals and events. Indeed, meeting community goals, or solving important problems is a requirement for institutional status. Even when events exist to create public good, such as promoting a cause or raising charitable donations, their goals and very existence might be contested by stakeholders who disagree with the cause (there are numerous controversial causes) or who reject the legitimacy of the organizers (usually for historical reasons, such as ethnic conflicts, or because of a clash of values or political positions). Legitimacy cannot be taken for granted.

Richards and Palmer (2010, p. 178), referring to the work of a national body, Event Scotland, said: "Legitimacy for the strategies is based on the involvement of major national bodies in its formulation. By gathering the key stakeholders behind the strategy and implicating them in the formulation of the mission, the resources necessary to undertake the strategy can also be mobilized." Williams and Elkhashab (2012) studied how social capital was generated by the Vancouver Olympic Winter Games, in particular the work of the Olympic tourism consortium – a network of stakeholders intended to leverage benefits from the mega-event. They found that the Consortium became "the legitimate single voice for tourism stakeholders" (p. 330) and it became more effective as the trust of the organizing committee was gained, thereby facilitating access to their vast stakeholder network.

Larson, Getz, and Pastras (2015) examined legitimacy in the events sector and concluded that it can be permanent or situational. They concluded (p. 170): "It has been argued that festival legitimacy is built and sustained within the culture of a local community, that a festival comes to be regarded as an institution" in terms of widespread and permanent legitimacy, and that the sources of legitimacy lie in moral authority, commercial success, legal status, and/or management strategy." Larson, Getz and Pastras (2015) formulated 13 propositions based on literature review and examples from their own research. These can have value in theory building but also may be used by practitioners as guidelines. They embody the various notions of how legitimacy is formed, and this is also a typology of forms of legitimacy.

Table 2.1: Legitimacy in the events sector. Reproduced with permission of Cognizant Communication, from the article by Larson et al. (2015).

☐ **Proposition 1:** Legal legitimacy does not ensure that moral or practical legitimacy will follow; legitimacy can be context specific, and will likely vary among stakeholders. Ownership by government agencies provides an instant degree of legitimacy that those in the private and nonprofit sectors have to earn.

☐ **Proposition 2:** Festivals, as a class or sector, generally possess a high degree of moral legitimacy owing to their perceived positive roles in building culture, the economy, and communities. Festivals in the not-for-profit and public sectors will more easily gain moral legitimacy than for-profit festivals because they are perceived to act for public service.

☐ **Proposition 3:** Although festivals are often viewed as vehicles of discourse, conflicting values can act to reduce legitimacy with respect to some stakeholders.

☐ **Proposition 4:** The media can positively or negatively influence the perceived legitimacy of festivals; therefore, it is important to foster close and positive media relations.

☐ **Proposition 5:** Within the "political market square" that describes a festival's network, legitimacy is linked mostly to trust; trust needs to be earned through transparency, accountability, shared decision making, and inclusiveness.

☐ **Proposition 6:** Festivals that create and sustain mutually rewarding exchanges with stakeholders will increase their pragmatic legitimacy.

☐ **Proposition 7:** Festival failure is linked to inadequate resources and the absence of uncommitted stakeholders; therefore, festivals that implement strategies for acquiring, sustaining, and regaining legitimacy should be more successful.

☐ **Proposition 8:** To a degree, legitimacy is manageable through communicative interaction with stakeholders, with regard to both conflict resolution and consensus building.

☐ **Proposition 9:** Effective leadership facilitates legitimacy, especially when leaders or other festival supporters are in themselves respected and trusted.

☐ **Proposition 10:** The lengthy process of becoming a permanent institution in a given community implies a high degree of cognitive legitimacy among the most important stakeholders, especially local government. Legitimacy is often a consequence of historical events; therefore, older festivals will generally hold greater legitimacy than new ones.

☐ **Proposition 11:** Large attendance and prestige will potentially generate higher levels of legitimacy owing to perceived success.

☐ **Proposition 12:** Longer-term relationships foster mutual respect and thereby increase reciprocal legitimacy.

☐ **Proposition 13:** Networks, or the entire festival sector, are often legitimized as instruments of public policy, giving rise to structural legitimacy.

Research notes

Yaghmour, S., & Scott, N. (2009). Inter-organizational collaboration characteristics and outcomes: A case study of the Jeddah Festival. *Journal of Policy Research in Tourism, Leisure and Events*, 1 (2), 115–130.

Abstract: Past research has found that a number of the characteristics of stakeholder collaboration are important in achieving desired group and individual outcomes. While these studies have identified various relationships between individual characteristics and selected outcomes, there has been little research on the relative importance of, and interaction between, collaboration characteristics. This research addresses this gap and examines the perceptions of event stakeholders in the Jeddah Festival (JF) held annually in Jeddah, Saudi Arabia, regarding the characteristics of collaboration and the collaborative outcomes perceived as important. The research uses content analysis of transcribed interviews conducted with JF stakeholders to identify the characteristics of stakeholder collaboration and collaborative outcomes. A correlation analysis between counts of the various characteristics and outcomes found in the transcripts was then conducted using a Spearman rank correlation. The results identified that governance and trust were the characteristics with the highest correlation with both individual and collective outcomes. This was interpreted as highlighting the perceived importance of these two collaboration characteristics for achieving festival outcomes. The research found that the nature of the collaborative environment is positive in part due to the initial legitimatization process and also due to survivor bias. Overall these findings provide evidence of the interaction between stakeholder collaboration characteristics and outcomes in the JF and provide guidance for how this collaboration may be improved.

Keywords: collaboration; outcomes; stakeholders; events; Saudi Arabia

Xue, H. & Mason, D.S. (2011). The changing stakeholder map of Formula
One Grand Prix in Shanghai. *European Sport Management Quarterly*, **11**(4),
371-395.

Abstract: In recent years, Formula One Auto Racing Grand Prix (F1) in Shanghai
has been dramatically impacted by the global recession and changes to the local
and national political-economic landscape. Due to the short lifespan of the event
(from 2004 through 2010), and the drastic changes that have occurred, F1 Shanghai provides a unique case to examine the manner through which the importance of stakeholders in a sport event environment change. Using Mitchell, Agle
and Wood's (1997) model, the current study develops two different stakeholder
maps of the F1 Shanghai event. In doing so, salience changes precipitated by
the turmoil occurring within the industry are assessed. By developing different stakeholder maps in different time periods, event organizers and managers
may better understand the dynamics of stakeholder interests and relationships,
which will be useful as event managers develop corresponding strategies to cope
with stakeholder changes in future events.

Keywords: Events; auto racing; stakeholder theory; China

Events as legitimacy-building tools

There are many examples of events being used to build or reinforce the legitimacy of specific interest groups, sub-cultures or causes. This is a case of stakeholder management in the sense that it entails an organization and its external
relationships, with image or perceived legitimacy as the main concerns of some.

A crisis of legitimacy

Tourism and events often provoke opposition, or are contested in terms of meaning and importance. Organizations seeking a social license to operate might find
that they are, instead, lacking in legitimacy in the minds of certain stakeholder
groups. As discussed by Habermas (1975), there is a general 'crisis of legitimacy'
in the modern world resulting from a perceived lack of citizen power, the widen-
ing gap between rich and poor, and the failure of institutions or governments to
deliver justice. Organizations are therefore often compelled to go the extra mile
to bring residents and other stakeholders into the decision-making process.

Contested events

While tourism in general is controversial in many places, including regulatory
actions against over-tourism, events are often focal points of contested values
and sometimes provide a forum for demonstrations and open conflict. The
meanings attached to celebrations and commemorations can be contested even
within the communities or cultures producing them, and therefore sensitivity

to varying stakeholder claims is warranted. How conflict is to be resolved, or avoided, is partly a matter of inclusion, as groups left out of decision-making are more likely to become opponents. On the other hand, some claims to be heard or to influence decisions will almost certainly result in a standoff.

Legitimation of events

The term 'legitimation' is used in a specific way within organizational ecology theory. Types of organizations that gain acceptance or are perceived to be legitimate in their functioning tend to grow in numbers, and this has been demonstrated in the context of festivals in Norway (Andersson, Getz, & Mykletun, 2013). The main check on growth is competition for resources, with successful events finding a niche that ensures them of continued demand and resources.

There is no doubt that around the world events of all types have been accepted as legitimate forms of entertainment, cultural expression, business and self or group expression, but they have also been instrumentalized by governments and corporations to meet many policy and strategic aims. The implication is that one has to look carefully at planned events to determine exactly what is their mandate and goals, and which stakeholders are possibly exploiting them for their own purposes.

2.7 Identifying and classifying event and tourism stakeholders

Within the events-specific literature the identification and classification of event stakeholders has been widely reported. Figure 2.3 is adapted from a paper by Getz, Andersson and Larson (2007) based on a comparative study of festivals in Calgary, Canada, and in Sweden. That paper makes it clear that there is a dynamic stakeholder environment with changing and overlapping stakeholder roles.

This modified diagram categorizes stakeholders according to the roles they play in events and event tourism, not just festivals. Keep in mind that local governments are often key regulators and facilitators, can also be producers of events, and typically own important venues. Local governments are also frequently involved with tourism and can be members or co-owners of DMOs and event development or bidding corporations. From a city and tourism perspective there are likely multiple event portfolios managed for different goals, and some level of collaboration among them is highly desirable.

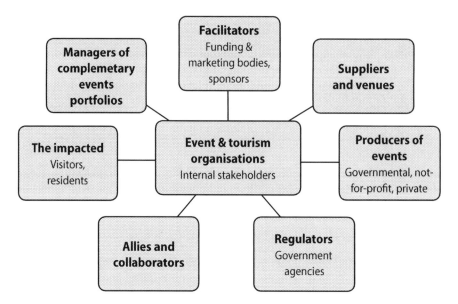

Figure 2.3: Stakeholders and their roles related to events and tourism. Source: Adapted from Getz et al. (2007)

There are always **internal stakeholders** including some or all of owners/investors, directors, employees, volunteers, members and advisors. 'Members' can be those who belong to societies or clubs, and 'advisors' are the professionals like accountants and lawyers who are retained for a fee, but provide ongoing and essential advice.

In the festivals research, 'co-producers' were independent organizations or businesses that are essential in producing the event, such as when a group of not-for-profits voluntarily collaborate to produce an event for mutual benefit. They might be indispensable to the event, providing services (like food and beverage or entertainers), volunteers, and co-branding. In Figure 2.3 however, this category has been changed to 'producers', a category that includes all the governmental, private and not-for-profit organizations that produce events – or can produce or support events. This can be called the 'events sector' and it generates events that belong to one or more managed event portfolios and taken together constitute the 'event population'.

Allies and collaborators have a less formal and often less tangible role to play than co-producers. They can be marketing allies, like tourism agencies, or professional festival and artist groups that support events politically (as lobbyists), provide volunteers, or share expertise and tangible resources. There is always a question of whether or not to count competitors as stakeholders. Whether they have a legitimate claim to be heard or involved is not always clear, because while competition for resources is a threat, destinations and events often cooperate in marketing or work together in other ways. The media might also be included here, but their role is not always supportive – it can be highly critical. Where appropriate, various media outlets can be brought into the category of internal stakeholders by making them long-term sponsors and co-marketers.

Facilitators hold power by virtue of providing money and other resources. Local government is a frequent financial supporter of festivals and events, while most events are also constantly working to increase financial and in-kind support from sponsors and foundations. Resources also include political and media support, and if it disappears or turns negative trouble will follow.

Suppliers and venues are essential to events, but their roles are not always purely commercial in nature. Venues sell their space to events, but they are also frequently producers of their own events; many arenas, theatres, concert halls, and stadia actively book shows, requiring links with agencies. Non-traditional venues include zoos, heritage sites, parks and museums. Suppliers of food, beverage, merchandise, labour, equipment and other services are vital, but they can be brought into the event organization by becoming sponsors or event co-producers. This strategy of internalizing stakeholders will often solve problems and enlarge the influence of organizers, but of course it results in a more complex set of inter-dependencies. From the perspective of DMOs, members are often the primary intended beneficiary. This category is the tourism and hospitality industry, with hotels, restaurants, retailers, venue owners, destination management companies etc. being highly involved in promotion and setting strategy.

Regulators hold power, including health and safety, building and fire, police and land use. Often these are departments of local government, so that politicians are both giving money and other support while overseeing the regulators who impose conditions and costs and sometimes preventing events. Event and tourism organizations cannot afford to have poor relationships with local government.

Managers of complementary event portfolios might be local government agencies such as leisure, sport, arts and culture, or collaborations of venues or not-for-profits. The main challenge is to look for common goals and pursue mutually reinforcing strategies. The larger the event population the more likely it is that conflicts occur as a result of normal ecological forces, especially competition for resources – money, audiences, sponsors, volunteers, venues, etc.

Finally, we have the **Impacted** category. The audience is the most obvious constituency, and their experience is of primary concern to event managers. This is especially true when the audience is fee-paying and the revenue from sales is necessary for financial viability. But the audience is drawn from the local community and beyond, so all residents become part of target marketing. And residents can and do support or oppose events or raise objections about perceived negative impacts.

Research notes: Tourism stakeholders

As revealed in the general tourism literature, stakeholders are vital to tourism development and destination management and marketing. In the following research notes the first authors, Sheehan and Ritchie (2005) identified destination stakeholders and their salience to the CEOs of North American destination organizations. Byrd and Gustke (2007) employed decision-tree analysis in South Carolina to examine stakeholder involvement in sustainable tourism planning. Presenza and Cipollina (2010) employed network analysis on a large sample of Italian hospitality firms, focusing on the preference for collaboration.

Sheehan, L. & Ritchie, J.R.B. (2005). Destination stakeholders: Exploring identity and salience. *Annals of Tourism Research*, **32** (3), 711-734.

Abstract: This paper applies a stakeholder theory analysis to the empirical study of chief executive officers of tourism destination management organizations. A map reveals a great diversity of varyingly important stakeholders. They are specifically analyzed within a typology according to their potential to threaten and cooperate with the organizations, then prescribing a management strategy specific to each. These strategies are compared to the actual approaches the respondent chief executive officers reported using. The paper concludes with an agenda for future empirical research with specific emphases on the relationship between destination management organizations and their stakeholders.

Keywords: stakeholder theory, destination management.

Byrd, E. & Gustke, L. (2007). Using decision trees to identify tourism stakeholders: The case of two Eastern North Carolina counties. *Tourism and Hospitality Research* **7**, 176-193.

Abstract: This paper explores stakeholder involvement in tourism planning, development, and management. For tourism planners to include stakeholders in the planning process, those stakeholders and their interests need to be identified. The research describes and applies an analytical technique that is not traditionally used to identify stakeholders. A questionnaire was developed and mailed to stakeholders in two rural communities in North Carolina. The data were analyzed with an Exhaustive Chi-square Automatic Interaction Detection decision tree. From the results of this, stakeholder groups were identified in relation to their support for sustainable tourism development in their community.

Keywords: decision tree analysis, stake-holder inclusion, sustainable tourism, tourism planning

Presenza, A. & Cipollina, M. (2010). Analyzing tourism stakeholders' networks. *Tourism Review*, **65** (4), 17-30.

Abstract: *Purpose* – The purpose of this paper is to analyze the variety of relations existing in tourism networks, identified as complex and mutable entities, where a vast range of stakeholders coexists.

Design/methodology/approach – After a deep review on stakeholder theory, the research applies techniques of network analysis to a case study. Specifically, the analysis focuses on 354 hospitality firms acting in Molise Region (Italy). Each operator was asked to judge the importance to collaborate with other stakeholders to enhance the effectiveness of their management and marketing activities. The answers highlight the degree of preference among stakeholders and the resulting information is the level of confidence in the network.

Findings – Results confirm the importance of intensifying relationships between tourism companies themselves and between them and policy makers. It appears that public stakeholders are more important for both management and marketing activities than private sector, since they place a much higher position in the scale of preference.

Research limitations/implications – The paper provides a starting-point for further research about non-quantitative destination performance measurement, such as trust and commitment between the stakeholders in tourism destination, and the use of network analysis' techniques.

Practical implications – Destination managers and policy-makers may use techniques of network analysis to elaborate useful information for planning and managing the relationships inside the tourism network.

Originality/value – The paper offers a novel approach for developing network analysis in tourism network literature. It explores non-quantitative destination performance measurements and uses management and marketing activities to analyze relationships between public and private stakeholders.

Keywords: Tourism management, tourism, partnership, stakeholder analysis

Discussion questions

1 Differentiate between the descriptive/empirical, instrumental, managerial, and normative perspectives on stakeholder theory.

2 Explain the Clarkson Principles in the context of Corporate Social Responsibility (CSR).

3 Describe Carroll's CSR Pyramid Model adapted and modified for events and tourism.

4 Define and give examples of primary and secondary stakeholders and active and passive stakeholders.

5 Give an example to explain stakeholder salience (combining power, legitimacy, and urgency) in the context of events and tourism.

6 How are an event's stakeholders and their roles likely to differ when the context is tourism planning at the destination level?

Assessment activities

Choose a planned event in your area (sports event, music festival, conference). Do a role-play exercise by taking on different stakeholders' roles (organizer, facilitator, supplier, regulator, visitor etc.) for each group member and discussing relationships between stakeholders. Each group should state why they see themselves as a stakeholder in the event and the reason for their involvement.

Additional readings and resources

Richards, G., & Palmer, R. (2010). *Eventful Cities.* Oxford: Butterworth Heinemann.

References

Andersson, T. & Getz, D. (2007). Resource dependency, costs and revenues of a street festival. *Tourism Economics*, **13** (1), 143-162.

Andersson, T. D., Getz, D. & Mykletun, R. J. (2013). Sustainable festival populations: An application of organizational ecology. *Tourism Analysis*, **18**(6), 621-634.

Byrd, E. & Gustke, L. (2007). Using decision trees to identify tourism stakeholders: The case of two Eastern North Carolina counties. *Tourism and Hospitality Research*, **7**, 176-193.

Carroll, A.B. (1993). *Business and Society: Ethics and Stakeholder Management,* 2nd Edn. Cincinnati: South-Western.

Caux Round Table for Moral Capitalism. (2018). Retrieved from http://www.cauxroundtable.org/index.cfm?&menuid=61

Clarkson, M. (1995). A stakeholder framework for analyzing and evaluating corporations. *Academy of Management Review*, **20**, (1), 92-118.

Donaldson, T. & Preston, L. (1995). The stakeholder theory of the corporation: Concepts, evidence and implications. *Academy of Management Review*, **20** (1), 65-91.

Getz, D. & Andersson, T. (2008). Sustainable festivals: On becoming an institution. *Event Management*, **12**, 1-17.

Getz, D., T. Andersson, & M. Larson (2007). Festival stakeholder roles: Concepts and case studies. *Event Management*, **10** (2/3), 103-122.

Habermas, J., (1975). *Legitimation Crisis,* translated by Thomas McCarthy. Beacon Jepson, A., Clarke, A., & Ragsdell, G. (2012). Investigating the use of the Motivation – Opportunity – Ability (MOA) model to reveal the factors which facilitate or inhibit inclusive engagement within local community festivals. *Global Events Congress: Conference proceedings*, Stavanger, Norway

Jepson, A., Clarke, A., & Ragsdell, G. (2014). Investigating the application of the motivation–opportunity–ability model to reveal factors which facilitate or inhibit inclusive engagement within local community festivals. *Scandinavian Journal of Hospitality and Tourism*, **14** (3), 331-348.

Jones, K. (2018). Gold Coast 2018 Commonwealth Games by numbers. Retrieved from: http://statements.qld.gov.au/Statement/2018/5/1/gold-coast-2018-commonwealth-games-by-numbers

Larson, M., Getz, D. & Pastras, P. (2015). The legitimacy of festivals and their stakeholders: concepts and propositions. *Event Management*, **19**(2), 159-174. DOI: dx.doi.org/10.3727/152599515X14297053839539 E-ISSN 1943-4308)

Mitchell, R., Agle, B.R. and Wood, D.J. (1997). Toward a theory of stakeholder identification and salience: defining the principle of who and what really counts. *Academy of Management Review*, **22** (4): 853–886.

Parent, M. M., & Deephouse, D. L. (2007). A case study of stakeholder identification and prioritization by managers. *Journal of Business Ethics*, **75**(1), 1-23.

Parsons, T. (1960) *Structure and Process in Modern Societies*. New York: Free Press.

Pham, T.D., Jin, C.X, Naranpanawa, A., Bandaralage, J. & Carmingnani, F. (2018). The economic impacts of the Gold Coast 2018 Commonwealth Games. Retrieved from: https://www.embracing2018.com/sites/default/files/gc-2018-economic-benefits-griffith-uni-report.pdf

Ponsford, I, & Williams, P. (2010). Crafting a social license to operate: a case study of Vancouver 2010's cypress Olympic venue. *Event Management*, **14** (1), 17-36.

Presenza, A. & Cipollina, M. (2010). Analyzing tourism stakeholders' networks. *Tourism Review*, **65** (4). 17-30.

Richards, G. & Palmer, R. (2010). *Eventful Cities*. Oxford: Butterworth Heinemann.

Sheehan, L., & Ritchie, J. R. B. (2005). Destination stakeholders: Exploring identity and salience. *Annals of Tourism Research*, **32** (3), 711-734.

Suchman, M. C. (1995). Managing legitimacy: Strategic and institutional approaches. *Academy of management review*, **20**(3), 571-610.

The Stanford Encyclopedia of Philosophy. (2016). Retrieved from https://plato.stanford.edu/entries/foucault/

Tiew, F., Holmes, K. & De Bussy, N. (2015). Tourism events and the nature of stakeholder power. *Event Management*, **19**, 525-541.

Williams, P. & Elkhashab, A. (2012). Leveraging tourism social capital: The case of the 2010 Olympic tourism consortium. *International Journal of Event and Festival Management*, **3**(3), 317–334.

Williams, P., Gill, A., Marcoux, J. & Xu, N. (2012). Nurturing 'social license to operate' through corporate-civil relationships in tourism destinations. In C. Hsu and W. Gartner (eds.), *The Routledge Handbook of Tourism Research*, pp. 196-214. London: Routledge.

Xue, H. & Mason, D.S. (2011). The changing stakeholder map of Formula One Grand Prix in Shanghai. *European Sport Management Quarterly*, **11**(4), 371-395.

Yaghmour, S. & Scott, N. (2009). Inter-organizational collaboration characteristics and outcomes: A case study of the Jeddah Festival. *Journal of Policy Research in Tourism, Leisure and Events*, **1** (2), 115–130

3 Generic Stakeholder Management Strategies

Learning objectives

At the end of the chapter readers should be able to:

☐ Design the continuous planning process for stakeholder management: where to start with stakeholder theory

☐ Determine which questions to ask during the process about internal and external stakeholders

☐ Discuss how to do a SWOT analysis

☐ Perform stakeholder mapping

☐ Classify stakeholders according to legitimacy, power and urgency, and their interest and ability to influence or collaborate with the focal organization

☐ Formulate a stakeholder strategy

☐ Evaluate a blended strategy matrix

☐ Understand the purpose of stakeholder contracts

3.1 Introduction

A continuous planning process for stakeholder management is described. To get started, and even for organizations already engaged with stakeholders, a set of questions is provided concerning internal and external stakeholders. A SWOT analysis might help, looking at the strengths, weaknesses, opportunities and threats attached to each stakeholder or type of stakeholder. A third planning technique is stakeholder mapping, described for both internal and external use.

A number of generic approaches to formulating strategy are reviewed, and they each take a somewhat different approach to classifying stakeholders and identifying appropriate strategies for managing relationships. From these we have provided a blended strategy matrix, but users will have to settle on their own approach appropriate to their circumstances.

3.2 Key terms defined

Event portfolio

"A full portfolio will consist of various types of events, for different target markets, held in different places, and at different times of the year, in pursuit of multiple goals." (Getz, 2013, p. 23).

"An event portfolio is the strategic patterning of disparate but interrelated events taking place during the course of a year in a host community that as a whole is intended to achieve multiple outcomes through the implementation of joint event strategies." (Ziakas, 2013, p. 14).

Focal organization

"The focal organization, the focus of the study, is an organized group with specific production and strategic goals that are justified by its mission, or raison d'être." West & Milio (2004).

KPIs

*"A **Key Performance Indicator** (KPI) is a measurable value that demonstrates how effectively a company is achieving key business objectives. Organizations use key performance indicators at multiple levels to evaluate their success at reaching targets. High-level KPIs may focus on the overall performance of the enterprise, while low-level KPIs may focus on processes or employees in departments such as sales, marketing or a call center."* Klipfolio Inc. (2018).

Stakeholder mapping

"Stakeholder mapping is the visual representation of a stakeholder analysis, organizing those people according to the key criteria with which you will be managing them during the project." Smartsheet Inc. (2018).

SWOT analysis

"SWOT (strengths, weaknesses, opportunities and threats) analysis is a framework for identifying and analyzing the internal and external factors that can have an impact on the viability of a project, product, place or person." Tech Target (2018).

3.3 Case study – Aardklop National Arts Festival, Potchefstroom, South Africa

(https://aardklop.co.za)

Elmarie Slabbert and Chris de Bruyn, North West University, South Africa

Aardklop (literally meaning something like 'Pulse of the Earth') National Arts Festival was established in 1998 to mainly serve the broader arts community in the northern half of South Africa and is hosted in Potchefstroom. The festival is one of the five big arts festivals in South Africa which offers a variety of Afrikaans productions in both performing and visual arts. The first festival started with just over 15,000 visitors, and this has steadily grown to over 150,000 per year.

Aardklop National Arts festival has however experienced significant changes which influenced the management of this festival. In 2016, after 18 years of existence, it was announced by the board of directors of Aardklop that the festival would be terminated with immediate effect in its current format. This was based on the question raised by the Chairperson of the Aardklop Foundation whether the festival is the best vehicle to support the arts in the current environment? It was time to rethink, be creative and innovative and remain focused on quality. But this was almost the end of the festival…

However, a number of influential people and groups in the Potchefstroom community, those with an interest in arts as well as previous sponsors of Aardklop convened in 2016 and decided to continue with the festival due to its economic and social contribution to arts and the community. At that time, it was labeled as the 'Potchefstroom Arts Festival,' and the new festival manager was appointed for the 2016 festival. It was thus back to the drawing board from 2016. This festival, although smaller, was a huge success and the enthusiasm of the organizing team made all the difference. The name of the festival was a sensitive matter but the board of directors negotiated for the continuous use of 'Aardklop National Arts Festival,' with the Aardklop Foundation and since 2017 it was promoted as such. The festival won the Fiesta-award for the Most Popular Arts Festival in 2017 and it is expected to grow significantly! The success of this festival is however dependent on stakeholders and their continued interest and support.

Photo 3.1: Aardklop National Arts Festival. Source: http://arttimes.co.za/aardklop-takes-a-new-direction/

Different stakeholders for the event

A number of stakeholders have an interest in this festival and these can be categorised as internal and external stakeholders.

Internal stakeholders

◆ **Board of Directors:** The purpose of the board of directors is to oversee the management of the Festival, to guide direction and ensure sound financial governance.

◆ **Permanent staff:** Aardklop hosts a festival office close to the location of the Festival, managed and organised by a festival manager, operational manager, a coordinator for sponsors, media and marketing, a coordinator for the festival terrain, a coordinator for the logistics and a program assistant.

◆ **Temporary staff**: Some temporary staff is hired during the festival to assist especially with servicing of venues, the festival terrain and overall administrative management.

External stakeholders

◆ **Sponsors**: The current sponsors are divided into nine categories with the companies ranging from local to national sponsors with an interest in arts. Besides sponsors that provide financial incentives, there are also organisations sponsoring specific products or services and projects. The festival has over 30 sponsors.

◆ **Local government**: The local government plays a crucial role in providing facilities and services during the time of the festival.

◆ **SAPS and Emergency Services:** The presence of the South African Police Service and Emergency Services is required by law.

◆ **Directors and producers from production companies**: the festival provides a platform to showcase productions of a certain standard and it is important to have these companies on board.

◆ **Artists, singers, musicians, dancers, performers, actors, visual artists**: Without these people, the festival is not possible and it is also important to have the more prominent and popular performers on board as they attract a higher number of visitors. The festival also creates platforms for young and upcoming artists.

◆ **Service providers**: They are essential stakeholders that provide key services to the festival including electricity distribution and cleaning services on the festival terrain, security at all the venues and technical production services (sound, lighting and staging) for all the productions in the different venues.

◆ **Stall holders/vendors/exhibitors**: A large number (±500) of stall holders/vendors/exhibitors are allowed to showcase and sell their products and services at the festival, as this also attracts visitors.

◆   **Local businesses**: These, especially the ones surrounding the festival terrain benefit from the festival and this serves as a financial boost for them.

◆   **Local tourism and hospitality establishments**: Given the number of visitors that overnight for this five-day festival, these establishments are directly benefitting from the event.

◆   **The local community (public) of Potchefstroom**: The festival is both economically and socially important to the local community as they benefit from hosting this type of event.

◆   **All festival goers/attendees/supporters**: The festival is not possible without the support of the attendees. The product must, however, attract these stakeholders and it is important to increase the numbers annually.

The process followed to identify the stakeholders

An in-depth stakeholder analysis was done by determining the following:

◆   The first phase was to conduct a complete product analysis to determine what is offered, how it is offered and who are currently involved.

◆   The second phase was to determine who should be involved in the festival, who are impacted by the festival and who impacts on the festival.

This led to the identification of the different internal and external stakeholders to be communicated and negotiated with.

The importance of stakeholder groups

All the stakeholders are important to the sustainability of the festival, but there is a large group of stakeholders without whom the festival cannot take place, simply because they play a key role in the management, finance and execution of the festival. They include:

◆   The staff

◆   Sponsors

◆   Local Government (for essential service delivery)

◆   The SAPS an EMRS (for legal compliance)

◆   The artists and performers

◆   All festival goers/attendees/supporters

Involvement of the stakeholders

The involvement of the stakeholders is based on the product analysis of the festival and determining the different stakeholders with a specific focus on the role that they play in the festival context, their contributions and the terms of their impact on the festival. Their involvement was enhanced with different strategies. For the sponsors, for example, a personal selling approach was followed where terms and conditions were negotiated. That also led to the categorisation of sponsors. For the local community, the opportunity was created to give direct input into the festival program through an artistic advisory committee that assisted in evaluating productions applying to be presented at the festival. For the local businesses, for example, the taxi industry, the opportunity was afforded to get involved by delivering transport services between the different venues to the festival goers. For the festival goers, an integrated marketing approach was followed to increase the interest and involvement. The focus was on a program launch held in Potchefstroom and Johannesburg. This stakeholder group was informed via the website of the program, debut productions, etc. For 2018 an app was developed where the festival goer can book tickets for shows and obtain up-to-date information on the festival.

Challenges with stakeholders

One of the biggest challenges in today's economic climate, especially in South Africa, is securing sustainable sponsorships for arts festivals. This is a process of constant negotiation, building relationships and enhancing networks. Second, it is challenging to get the local government on board as priorities might differ. It was important that they understand the economic gains from this festival to secure their support. One cannot host this type of festival without their support since the facilities and services that they provide are used.

Specific focus on the local community where the event took place

Although this festival has a national footprint and mainly focusses on serving the broader arts community in the northern half of South Africa, several aspects in the planning and execution of this festival were focused on the local community. This included amongst others:

♦ Pre-ticket sales to the local community before sales opened for the rest of the country.

♦ Awarding the majority of tenders to local service providers for services needed during the festival.

♦ Recruiting ±300 temporary staff for the festival week directly from the local community.

♦ Taking certain festival program elements to previously disadvantaged parts of the community so they can share in the festival experience and benefits.

♦ Creating a dedicated venue for local artists to give them an opportunity to perform at the festival.

♦ Making space available on the festival grounds for local crafters to exhibit and sell their works of art.

The management of the stakeholders

For each stakeholder group, a strategy was developed to address their needs. This is an intense process as all stakeholders are important in the delivery of a festival such as this one – it is thus an integrated effort depended on individual inputs. In general, the management of stakeholders was based on effective communication using direct communication channels and as many as possible of the social media platforms. Messages were tailor-made to fit the interests of specific groups. It was also necessary to communicate through individual stakeholder group meetings. The management of stakeholders is a continuous process happening, before, during and even after the event, especially in the case of a recurring event such as Aardklop.

Lessons learned from the stakeholder engagement

♦ One can never invest too much time in building stakeholder relationships.

♦ One can never communicate enough with all your stakeholders.

♦ LISTEN to your stakeholders and make sure you understand their needs.

♦ Do not over-promise and under-perform.

♦ Stakeholder management should be carefully planned and is a critical part of event management.

3.4   A planning process

As with all rational planning, a process can be suggested that starts with the organization's mandate (profit or service being the key considerations), considers its strategies, goals, and performance measures (or KPIs), then links stakeholder input and management to each of these. But that is likely to be too linear and static, because in reality stakeholder issues are arising all the time, in a complex, dynamic environment. No event can be created, or tourism agency operate for any length of time without having to deal with multiple stakeholders. Over time, a practical system will have emerged that addresses the main issues and manages the key relationships.

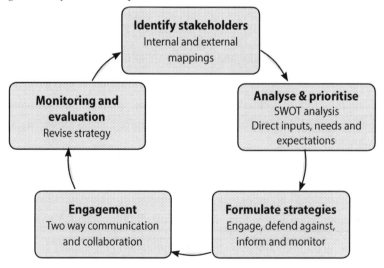

Figure 3.1: Continuous planning process for stakeholder management.

Figure 3.1 provides a model of a continuous or cyclical planning process with five main elements. The first is identification: who are they internally and externally? This can be done through a logical analysis, asking the questions found in Table 3.1. The second stage is analysis and prioritization, and this requires some research and/or direct input from the stakeholders themselves. A SWOT analysis and stakeholder mapping will be useful here. Strategies are formulated, at least for critical or primary stakeholders and these are discussed later in this chapter: monitor, inform, defend against or engage. Since many stakeholders will fall into the categories of primary and secondary (as opposed to those lacking in urgency or legitimacy) the fourth element in the process is engagement, and this involves both a two-way communications process and various forms of collaboration. As with all strategic planning models, monitoring the relationships and evaluating the management process will undoubtedly lead to revisions and hopefully to continuous improvements.

One good starting point is to ask some basic questions, and this is especially critical for events and organizations that have not previously been formally identifying and managing stakeholder issues.

3.4.1 Getting started: Questions to ask

Freeman (1984) suggested a set of questions to get started with the process of stakeholder management. We have placed these in the Table 3.1 and added event-related and tourism-related examples. This exercise is also necessary for stakeholder mapping, as discussed below.

Table 3.1: Questions to ask about external and internal stakeholders

Event-related	Tourism-related
Who are our current and potential stakeholders?	
In each category, who are they? Staff and volunteers; audiences; facilitators; regulators; suppliers/ venues; allies and collaborators; co-producers; impacted (e.g., residents)	In each category, who are they? DMO members; attractions; event organizations; travel services; media; government agencies; lobby groups; citizens
What are their interests/rights? Internal and external stakeholders?	
The right to a safe, healthy, work environment The expectation of value for money and satisfying or memorable experiences The right to legal, fair treatment The hope for sustainable operations and an enduring event The need for responsible finances	The expectation of accountability and transparency from politicians, members, partners and citizens (meaning full disclosure of finances, policies, strategies, actions and impacts) The expectation of socially responsible and environmentally sound strategies and practices The hope for economic prosperity for all (versus a narrow focus on business profit)

How does each stakeholder affect us?	
Roles can overlap and change: Are they suppliers? co-producers? facilitators? allies or collaborators? regulators? impacted? Events will fail without widespread support and perceived legitimacy	Members are generally crucial for financing and political support Residents and media can influence stakeholder and political support Tourists & potential markets critical to success Individual businesses in the destination can cause reputation damage or uphold a positive image and strong brand
How do we affect each stakeholder?	
Co-producers, suppliers, staff and volunteers are affected directly by the event as to health, safety, and financial viability Audiences are directly affected as to health, safety, comfort and satisfactory/memorable experiences Residents and others are affected directly some of the time (e.g. noise, traffic) or indirectly (taxes, leisure opportunities) The environment might be represented by regulators and lobbyists, with perceived or legal legitimacy	Businesses in general depend on effective strategy and marketing Members have a financial interest in success, and a legal right to sound management The public, represented by politicians, is impacted economically, socially, and environmentally by tourism and by the DMOs investments
What assumption does our current strategy make about each important stakeholder?	
Without explicit stakeholder management many assumptions will creep into policy and actions Obtain direct input through proactive engagement	
What are the environmental variables that affect us and our stakeholders?	
Consider competition, the management of event portfolios, and the health of the event population	Conduct research and a competitive SWOT evaluation to gain understanding of environmental forces and trends, especially those related to demand for the destination's products and experiences
How do we measure each of these variables and their impact?	
A comprehensive planning and evaluation system will incorporate direct input from, and results of research concerning stakeholders Set goals and key performance indicators	A comprehensive planning and evaluation system will incorporate direct input from, and results of research concerning stakeholders Set goals and key performance indicators
How do we keep score with our stakeholders?	
Joint planning and evaluation sessions Use the balanced scorecard or Event Compass evaluation systems	Transparent impact assessment and evaluations are essential for accountability Members have votes! Politicians have the ability to change support and regulations

Another possible starting point suggested by Freeman (1984) is to analyze stakeholder behavior (e.g., past action, trends), consider possible coalitions between stakeholders' groups, and assess any competitive threats. These are clearly strategic issues that might be examined by planners in preparation of a five-year plan, or as part of annual environmental scanning.

3.4.2 SWOT Analysis

A Strengths, Weaknesses, Threats and Opportunities analysis is often done in strategic planning, especially with regard to competitors, but it can be useful for helping develop strategies for any given stakeholder. The stakeholder in question can also be a group or category, such as suppliers or volunteers, but a more refined analysis will usually be desirable. For a competitor-oriented SWOT the boxes are to contain (as a result of analysis) important conditions or issues relative to the competitor – in other words, what are their strengths and weaknesses relative to us? But when used to assess other stakeholders – those with whom the focal organization has relationships other than competition – the four quadrants can include a wider range of characteristics and issues.

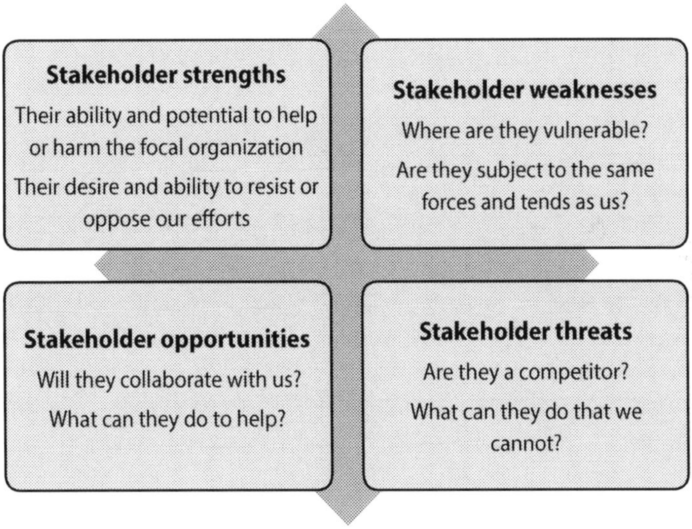

Stakeholder strengths

Their ability and potential to help or harm the focal organization

Their desire and ability to resist or oppose our efforts

Stakeholder weaknesses

Where are they vulnerable?

Are they subject to the same forces and tends as us?

Stakeholder opportunities

Will they collaborate with us?

What can they do to help?

Stakeholder threats

Are they a competitor?

What can they do that we cannot?

Figure 3.2: Sample SWOT analysis for stakeholders. Source: authors' contribution

In Figure 3.2 a few examples are given in each quadrant. Under 'Weaknesses', analysis should indicate where the stakeholder in question is vulnerable, and this might be a unique condition or something shared with the focal organization. For example, many festivals are likely to share the burden of debt or the necessity for lines of credit to continue operating, but some will be in a vulnerable dependency position because one funder or sponsor that withdraws support could, all on its own, cause event failure.

Under 'Strengths', look for characteristics that can help them endure and for the focal organization to take advantage of, through collaboration. Strengths might also include the ability of the stakeholder to resist or oppose, as some competitors will do, and an evaluation of their desire to help or hinder. This leads to threats, because even if a stakeholder has the potential to resist, oppose or harm that does not mean they will be a threat. A good question to ask is: "What can they do that we cannot?", which is another way of examining distinctive competencies, and leads to an assessment of whether or not that stakeholder might become a threat in the future. For 'Opportunities', the analysts are trying to identify some potential to exploit that is not currently visible, such as hypothetical scenarios in which collaboration might become possible or perhaps even a merger.

3.4.3 Stakeholder mapping

It is amazing how much information and dialogue will emerge when owners or managers are asked to identify their stakeholders and discuss relationships with them. The very act of doing this research, especially with a sketch, can lead to entirely new approaches to stakeholder management and strategic planning. And the 'map' does not have to be a diagram, it can be a table or a series of notes, all performing the same function.

One approach to constructing stakeholder maps is to hold a strategy meeting within the organization and ask the Freeman questions in Table 3.1. This can work for internal and external stakeholders but is really a first-cut effort that should lead to wide consultations. Another approach, or following from the internal mapping, is to reach out to key stakeholders and interview them, asking each one to describe their relationships with the event or tourism organization, and with other stakeholders (such as their supply chain or marketing partners). A 'snowball' technique will involve asking each interviewee to identify contacts for additional interviews, so the map will keep expanding – in terms of numbers of stakeholders – until, ideally, everyone has been accounted for. This approach will yield a fuller understanding of the relevant network, and especially how the event or tourism organization is perceived from outside. It can easily be combined with details enabling a network map and analysis – focusing on centrality, the strength of links, bridging organizations, and gaps.

Internal mapping

Internal stakeholders should already be known, but how is each category perceived and managed– what issues do they have with, say the owner or executive officer? How do staff and volunteers interact? Each internal stakeholder group should be consulted about internal relations, but it might also be useful to ask about their external relationships – the union, for example, might have a completely different perspective than managers about some external stakeholders.

Table 3.2: Mapping internal stakeholders – their primary concerns and influence

Primary concerns	Influence
Permanent paid staff	
Wages and benefits	Staff deliver service quality and form an important part of the experience
Safe, healthy, supportive working conditions	
Job security	Potential for labor strife & disruption of events
Satisfaction through meeting challenges and self-development	Requirement for permanent recruitment, training, performance evaluation.
Career advancement; preparation for other jobs.	CEOs and senior managers will often have control over operations
Part-time or casual employees	
Similar to permanent staff, but…	They require special recruitment, training and performance evaluation; might not gel with permanent staff or volunteers.
Seeking permanent employment?	
Might have multiple jobs and external responsibilities	
Volunteers	
Motivation can be a mix of altruism, seeking specific tangible benefits, self-development/actualization, skill acquisition, networking, socializing, commitment to a sport, cause or leisure pursuit.	Many events are entirely volunteer driven. Working conditions for volunteers and staff can be quite different, but both stakeholder groups are usually critical for event success.
Board of directors	
Volunteers will have somewhat different interests from paid/professional Directors.	Potential for conflict over strategy and policy. Essential to get a Board representative of all stakeholders/citizens.
Members or outsiders? (e.g., DMOs might secure Directors only from industry members, versus seeking external experts)	
Elected or appointed? (e.g., local government might require a seat on the board for a staff person or politician)	
Members (usually fee-paying and entitled to vote, but in not-for-profit organizations there can be voluntary membership without fees	
Members will demand sound management, full accountability (internally, at least), and fulfillment of the organization's mandate	Members are typically entitled to vote on Directors and to be consulted on strategy and policy
Boards are usually elected from within the membership, meaning that succession planning is important	When members are disappointed they can have officials replaced
Professional advisors	
Might be asked to volunteer and sit on the Board.	Their roles could be a mix of impartial advisor and supporter.

Internal stakeholders can be analyzed by identifying their primary concerns (these should not be merely assumed) and consideration of their influence on the organization, as illustrated in Table 3.2.

Mapping external stakeholders

In this exercise, recommended for every organization, the event or agency considers itself to be the 'focal organization' that is looking externally at its stakeholders. If a group of events and agencies do this at the same time (or an independent researcher takes it on), say within the context of evaluating a city or destination event portfolio, the 'big picture' of inter-organizational networks will emerge. Social network mapping will provide a similar and complementary overview, although that type of analysis does not usually address management issues.

Taking the point of view of a consultant or independent researcher who is interviewing managers, these questions can start the dialogue and lead to a 'map':

♦   Which of the following stakeholder groups are absolutely critical to your continued viability? (Assuming the interviewer already has a list)

♦   Why are some of them critical? (Prompting with these points: they provide resources/venues/supplies/performers/competitors; they are regulators; their opposition would be fatal, etc.);

♦   What are the issues?

♦   How do you deal with them?

♦   Which external stakeholders are important to you, but you could survive without them? (this is open-ended, and also a possible starting point); describe the issues that arise with each stakeholder; how are they managed?

♦   What other stakeholders have a legitimate claim to be consulted or to intervene? Why?

The interviewer might have to draw a diagram if the interviewee is reluctant or unable to do so. Follow these steps:

1   Draw a circle or square in the middle of a blank page and label it (this is the focal organization), but use the name of the event or agency.

2   Around this focal organization draw other circles/boxes for each mentioned stakeholder.

3   Connect the focal organization to the stakeholders using different kinds of lines or arrows (e.g., heavy lines indicate strong links or critical connections).

4   Connect interdependent stakeholders with each other, if the source knows which ones interact.

Additional questions not essential to the map, but for planning:

♦ Have you had problems with any of these stakeholders? Please discuss.

♦ How are all these relationships managed? How could they be improved?

♦ Looking ahead, what opportunities or threats can you foresee? Can you envisage any problems arising because certain groups feel left out or unheard?

♦ Have your important stakeholders given you a 'social license to operate'? That is, will they continue to support your event(s) and defend its purpose and goals?

♦ If your existence is threatened, who can you count on to come to your rescue?

A simple stakeholder map is illustrated in Figure 3.3; it could be drawn by a manager contemplating the event's main external and internal stakeholders, but this one uses categories rather than specific, named persons or organizations. A second level of detail would cover the specific suppliers, advisors, interest groups, etc. Modifying the lines or arrows could be used to indicate critical links, or strength of relationship. Note that lines between external stakeholders indicate important linkages that are somehow connected to the focal organization or event. In this illustration major inter-stakeholder links are shown for local government and the DMO or tourism organization, between allies/collaborators and co-producers, between sponsors and the audience, and between the audience and the impacted.

Stakeholder mapping and strategizing has to reflect the context, starting with the ownership and mandate of the organization. With a DMO as the focal organization the map would be different, with members (e.g., hotels, attractions, restaurants, retailers) becoming critical. The importance of links between local government and a tourism agency will depend in large part on whether or not government and industry share funding and policymaking, and the composition of the Board of Directors. Researchers Sheehan and Ritchie (2005) questioned CEOs of various North American destination marketing organizations and determined that their most salient stakeholders were hotels/hotel association, city/local government, regional/county government, attractions/attraction association, state/provincial tourism departments, and of course members of the DMO. In a map-making variation utilized by Sheehan and Ritchie (2005) the stakeholder map places stakeholders of high importance ('primary or critical') close to the focal organization and those with little salience at the outside of the diagram. This requires some additional measurement on a scale when multiple informants provide input, or a judgment on the part of whoever is preparing the analysis as to degrees of criticality. For many events and DMOs the major sources of funding would probably determine criticality, reflecting the answer to this question: "If stakeholder X withdrew all support could we survive?"

Figure 3.3 provides an illustration, really a starting point for adapting the mapping technique to various situations. A festival is the focal organization and its main stakeholders are in categories derived previously, from research. Critical or primary stakeholders are emphasized graphically by boxes and heavy lines. Links of importance between stakeholders are indicated by dashed lines. These inter-stakeholder links are really part of what a full network analysis would reveal, and they could be important to the festival. For example, regulators within local government are always critical, but the same politicians will often sit on the boards of DMOs or at least have a say in tourism policy and planning.

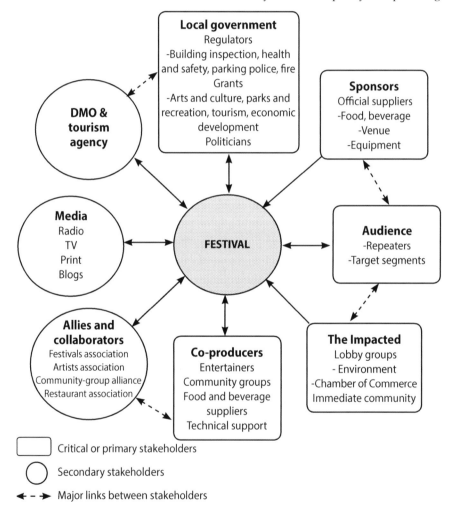

Figure 3.3: Sample external stakeholder map

The article by Amaral, Bastao and Carvalho (2018) is an excellent example of how event organizers have identified their stakeholders, determined their power and formed a strategy to manage them.

Research note

Amaral, C. D. S., Bastos, F. D. C., & Carvalho, M. M. (2018). Stakeholders mapping in sporting events projects: case study. *PODIUM: Sport, Leisure and Tourism Review,* 7(1), 22-45.

Abstract: Given the gap in stakeholder literature on the sports scene in the Brazilian context, the aim of this study was to examine how managers identify, ranks and prioritize the stakeholders of a sportsport event. For this purpose, a case study was conducted of the event 'Volta da USP' in its 52nd edition. Data were collected through semi-structured interviews with three managers from different levels of the project and with five stakeholders. The content analysis was conducted to verify the attributes power, legitimacy and urgency granted to stakeholders, classifying them into 7 types. It was possible to verify that there is a difference in identifying the stakeholders depending on the managers' organizational level. The most common attribute among the stakeholders was legitimacy. As for the types found, we identified stakeholders as permanently dependent, dominant, discretionary and inactive. Prioritization of stakeholders by managers yields a higher level of importance to those who have two or more attributes over those that have only one attribute.

Keywords: Community of Portuguese language countries, developing countries, Latin America, America, South America, threshold countries, Brazil

3.5 Formulating strategy

Consideration can be given to appropriate management strategies at any stage in the stakeholder planning process, although actual commitment to a strategy is not usually desirable until a full SWOT analysis and mapping is done. What might appear to be a good strategy for one stakeholder might turn out to be inefficient or otherwise unwise when the entire network of stakeholder relationships has been evaluated.

A number of strategies have been identified, and they are all structured as either a matrix or intersecting rings. Our blended adaptation of a stakeholder strategy matrix is in Figure 3.4, but users can select the best model or combination to suit their purpose.

3.5.1 Strategy matrix by Savage, Nix, Whitehead, and Blair

Savage et al. (1991) recommended evaluation of each stakeholder's potential for cooperation and potential to threaten, as illustrated in the adapted Figure 3.4. Those theorists labeled four categories as 'mixed blessing', 'nonsupportive', 'marginal' and 'supportive'. This approach is particularly useful when looking for partnerships.

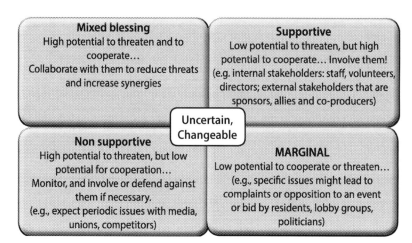

Figure 3.4: Mapping stakeholder's capacity to threaten. Adapted from Savage et al. (1991)

The recommended strategies have to be carefully considered. Collaboration is an obvious choice for events and event tourism, as much more can be achieved through collaboration than through direct competition, albeit within some constraints. But 'defend' is a strategy not to be taken lightly. If stakeholders are opposed, or a potential threat, it might be best to ask how their interests can be satisfied or appeased rather than attempt to keep them at bay or to minimize their influence. For example, some residents might threaten political action if noise is not reduced (or any other amenity issue), but should that issue be ignored or the noise pollution defended just because they are a small dissenting group?

3.5.2 The Winch matrix

A matrix by Winch (2004) can be used to classify stakeholders according to their influence and power (e.g., power over the event organizers) on the vertical axis and their interest level (which could be interpreted as the degree to which they are engaged, take notice or interfere) on the horizontal axis.

		Name of stakeholder	Number of stakeholders
Internal	Demand Side		
	Supply Side		
External	Private		
	Public		

Figure 3.5: Identify stakeholders for the organization. Adapted from Winch (2004)

Users can substitute other dimensions and classify stakeholders accordingly. For example, you could plot degree of financial/political support (vertical axis) against need for formal accountability (horizontal axis). In such a matrix, certain environmental lobby groups only need to be kept informed because they demonstrate (or are perceived) to offer no support but do require accountability on impacts; the local government's culture department might be a key funder and therefore must be fully engaged at all times.

Winch (2004) suggested strategies, but they depend on how one classifies stakeholders:

♦ **Monitor:** these stakeholders do not represent an urgent claim or problem, but might change to become more important or urgent; devise ways to learn about them and to filter information from the environment.

♦ **Keep them informed:** these stakeholders want to know what you are doing, or you owe them a degree of accountability; it can be the lack of communication that leads to problems for the event, such as failing to inform residents of changes in traffic.

♦ **Satisfy their needs:** they are important enough that you must know and meet their needs or demands, including regulators and those providing funds and other support.

♦ **Fully engage:** Some stakeholders are so powerful or influential that they should be brought into your operations and/or decision-making; can suppliers become sponsors and sponsors become directors or shareholders? Can unions be fully engaged as opposed to confrontation? Are politicians suspicious or hostile, and if so will engaging them change their attitudes or policies?

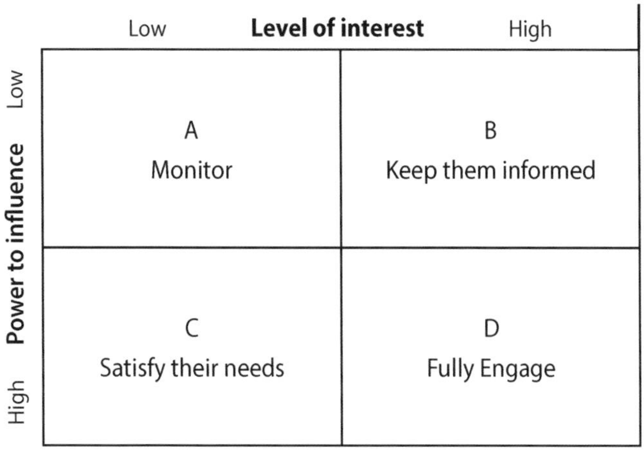

Figure 3.6: Mapping stakeholder's relative importance for the organization. Adapted from Winch (2004)

3.5.3 Power, legitimacy and urgency

Another approach is to use the legitimacy, power and urgency categorization to draw three intersecting rings yielding a more refined picture of stakeholders – with implications for how they should be managed (Boonstra, 2006; Mitchell et al., 1997). The resulting classification is:

♦ **Dormant** stakeholders: Possess power to impose their will but, not having a legitimate relationship or an urgent claim, their power remains unused.

♦ **Discretionary** stakeholders: Possess legitimacy, but have no power to influence and no urgent claim. There is no pressure to engage.

♦ **Demanding** stakeholders: Exist where the sole attribute is urgency: those with urgent claims, but have neither legitimacy nor power.

♦ **Dominant** stakeholders: Powerful and legitimate. Their influence in the relationship is assured and they can help form a dominant coalition.

♦ **Dependent** stakeholders: Lack of power, but have urgent and legitimate claims. They depend on others to carry out their will. Power in this relationship is not reciprocal and is advocated through the values of others.

♦ **Dangerous** stakeholders: Possess urgency and power but not legitimacy and may be coercive or dangerous. The use of coercive power often accompanies illegitimate status.

♦ **Definitive** stakeholders: Possess power, legitimacy, and urgency. Any stakeholder can become definitive by acquiring the missing attributes.

♦ **Non-stakeholders**: Possess none of the attributes and, thus, do not have any type of relationship with the group, organization or project.

Caution should be employed when classifying stakeholders this way, because a mistake could lead to bad management. For example, if a group is defined as a non-stakeholder, and ignored, it could take exception and try to disrupt the event. A valuable complement to this analysis would be to ask stakeholders themselves to describe their ideal relationships, and to ask impartial experts to evaluate the organization and its relationships. There is always a possibility that the researcher, planner or analyst is "too close to the trees to see the forest".

3.5.4 Lim's strategies

Lim et al. (2005) proposed a useful range of strategies:

♦ **Reactive**: deny any responsibility to accommodate their interests (this could be risky)

♦ **Defensive**: work with them only to the degree necessary (this might be necessary because resources are not adequate to do more)

♦ **Accommodative**: satisfy all their needs/demands; permanent relationships needed

♦ **Proactive**: do more than is required; identify them and get them engaged.

3.5.5 Freeman's strategies

Freeman (2010) distinguishes between four main strategies depending on the type of stakeholders:

♦ Take the '**offensive**' when a group is supportive; try to change stakeholder objectives or perceptions, adopt the stakeholder position, or link the program to others that the stakeholder views more favorably.

♦ Be '**defensive**' when a group is non-supportive; prevent competitive threats; reinforce current beliefs about the stakeholder, maintain existing programs or let the stakeholder drive the integration process.

♦ A '**swing**' strategy should be adopted when a group presents a 'mixed blessing'; take decisions such as changing the rules.

♦ '**Hold**' strategies should be adopted when a group is marginal; continue current strategy.

Research notes

Xue, H., & Mason, D.S. (2011). The changing stakeholder map of Formula One Grand Prix in Shanghai. *European Sport Management Quarterly*, **11**(4), 371-395.

Abstract: In recent years, Formula One Auto Racing Grand Prix (F1) in Shanghai has been dramatically impacted by the global recession and changes to the local and national political-economic landscape. Due to the short lifespan of the event (from 2004 through 2010), and the drastic changes that have occurred, F1 Shanghai provides a unique case to examine the manner through which the importance of stakeholders in a sport event environment change. Using Mitchell, Agle and Wood's (1997) model, the current study develops two different stakeholder maps of the F1 Shanghai event. In doing so, salience changes precipitated by the turmoil occurring within the industry are assessed. By developing different stakeholder maps in different time periods, event organizers and managers may better understand the dynamics of stakeholder interests and relationships, which will be useful as event managers develop corresponding strategies to cope with stakeholder changes in future events.

Keywords: Events; auto racing; stakeholder theory; China

Van Niekerk, M. (2016). The applicability and usefulness of the stakeholder strategy matrix for festival management. *Event Management*, **20**, 165–179.

Abstract: This article examines the applicability and usefulness of the stakeholder strategy matrix in the context of festival management. An extensive literature review gave rise to the development of an online survey. Data for the study were collected from festival managers in the US. This empirical study indicated that internal and external festival stakeholders differ from each other in significant ways, and that different management strategies should be used to manage them. The stakeholder strategy matrix appears to be more effective for the management of internal festival stakeholders and the least effective for managing external festival stakeholders. Based on the results of the study, it can be postulated that the stakeholder strategy matrix can be applied effectively towards managing festival stakeholders and may provide useful management strategies for festival managers when managing their internal and external stakeholders. This is one of the first studies to be conducted in this area, and as such it contributes to the body of knowledge on management strategies for internal and external festival stakeholders.

Keywords: Stakeholder theory; stakeholder strategy matrix; festivals; events; festival management

3.5.6 A blended stakeholder strategy model for events and tourism

Combining a typology of stakeholders with pertinent strategies in one diagram can lead to over-generalization, and also be quite messy. Given the range of categories and strategies discussed previously, we have prepared an example of what users can do within their own contexts and according to their own needs. This diagram (Figure 3.7) plots stakeholders according to increasing potential for collaboration (vertical axis) against increasing power and influence on the horizontal axis. These terms can be interpreted in different ways, so a working definition is required for each. Input could be in the form of stakeholder consultations and mapping or simply the judgment of whoever is producing the analysis. Note that there might very well be unknowns, or a grey area where mixed criteria yield confusion, and so a central box has been added; for these uncertainties a monitor and inform strategy makes sense.

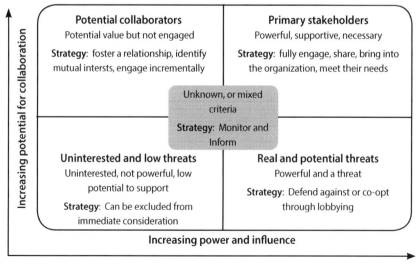

Figure 3.7: A blended strategy matrix for stakeholder management.

3.5.7 Contracts with stakeholders

If organizers and stakeholders believe in the concept of 'social license to operate', then some form of implicit or literal contract is made between organizations. Freeman (1994) suggested a 'doctrine of fair contracts' that would reflect the following principles:

♦ *The principle of entry and exit*: The contract has to define a process that clarifies entry, exit and renegotiation conditions for stakeholders to decide when an agreement can be fulfilled

♦ *The principle of governance:* Procedures for changing the rules of the game must be agreed by unanimous consent. This would lead to a stakeholder governing board.

♦ *The principle of externalities:* If a contract between A and B involves C, C has to be invited as a party of the contract.

♦ *The principle of contracting costs*: Each party must share in the cost of contracting

♦ *The agency principle*: Any party must serve the interests of all stakeholders

♦ *The principle of limited immortality*: The corporation should be managed as if it can continue to serve the interests of stakeholders through time.

Although most stakeholder relationships are unlikely to involve formal contracts, the Freeman principles do seem to cover what actually happens in member-based organizations like many DMOS, and in events produced by multiple parties (or co-producers). The analogy of the 'political market square' is also pertinent, with stakeholder legitimacy being a central issue when it comes to who is involved and who has power.

Discussion questions

1 When designing a planning process for an event's stakeholder management, what aspects of stakeholder theory should inform your planning?

2 What questions should you ask of internal and external stakeholders during the planning process?

3 Explain how to do a SWOT analysis and illustrate an example.

4 Illustrate a stakeholder map and explain how it is developed and used.

5 What is the logic behind a stakeholder classification based on legitimacy, power and urgency; define these terms.

6 What strategies are appropriate based on a stakeholder's interest and ability to influence or collaborate with the event organization?

7 Why is a flexible, blended strategy needed for events?

8 Discuss the purpose of stakeholder contracts and when they might be needed.

Assessment activities

Look up a website of your favorite international event and familiarize yourself with the event goals, objectives, target audience, and other characteristics. Draw a stakeholder map and discuss what strategies would work best to gain support from each stakeholder category.

Recommended additional readings and sources

Freeman, R. (2010). *Strategic Management: A stakeholder approach.* Cambridge MA: Cambridge University Press.

Ziakas, V. (2013). *Event Portfolio Planning and Management: A Holistic Approach.* Abingdon: Routledge.

References

Amaral, C. D. S., Bastos, F. D. C. & Carvalho, M. M. (2018). Stakeholders mapping in sporting events projects: case study. *PODIUM: Sport, Leisure and Tourism Review,* **7**(1), 22-45.

Boonstra, A. (2006). Interpreting an ERP-implementation project from a stakeholder perspective. *International Journal of Project Management,* 24(1), 38-52.

Freeman, R.E. (1984). *Strategic Management: A Stakeholder Approach.* Boston: Pitman.

Freeman, R. E. (1994). The politics of stakeholder theory: Some future directions. *Business Ethics Quarterly,* 409-421.

Freeman, R. E. (2010). *Strategic Management: A stakeholder approach.* Cambridge University Press.

Getz, D. (2013). *Event Tourism.* New York: Cognizant Communication Corp.

Klipfolio Inc. (2018). Retrieved from https://www.klipfolio.com/resources/articles/what-is-a-key-performance-indicator

Lim, G., Ahn, H. & Lee, H. (2005). Formulating strategies for stakeholder management: A case-based reasoning approach, *Expert Systems with Applications,* **28**, 831-840

Mitchell, R., Agle, B.R. & Wood, D.J. (1997). Toward a theory of stakeholder identification and salience: defining the principle of who and what really counts. *Academy of Management Review,* **22** (4): 853–886.

Savage, G., Nix, T., Whitehead, C. & Blair, J. (1991). Strategies for assessing and managing organizational stakeholders. *Academy of Management Executive,* **5** (2), 61-75.

Sheehan, L. & Ritchie, J. R. B. (2005). Destination stakeholders: Exploring identity and salience. *Annals of Tourism Research,* **32** (3), 711-734.

Smartsheet Inc. (2018) Retrieve from https://www.smartsheet.com/what-stakeholder-analysis-and-mapping-and-how-do-you-do-it-effectively

Tech Target. (2018). Retrieve from https://searchcio.techtarget.com/definition/ SWOT-analysis-strengths-weaknesses-opportunities-and-threats-analysis

Van Niekerk, M. (2016). The applicability and usefulness of the stakeholder strategy matrix for festival management. *Event Management*, **20**, 165–179.

West, V. L. & Milio, N. (2004). Organizational and environmental factors affecting the utilization of telemedicine in rural home healthcare. *Home health care services quarterly*, **23**(4), 49-67.

Winch, G.M. (2004). *Managing Construction Projects-An Information Processing Approach*. Blackwell Science.

Xue, H., & Mason, D.S. (2011). The changing stakeholder map of Formula One Grand Prix in Shanghai. *European Sport Management Quarterly*, **11**(4), 371-395.

Ziakas, V. (2013). *Event Portfolio Planning and Management: A Holistic Approach*. Abingdon: Routledge.

4 Applying Stakeholder Theory to the Management Functions

Learning objectives

By the end of the chapter, readers should be able to understand how to apply stakeholder theory to the following management functions:

- [ ] Organizing and planning
- [ ] Sustainability
- [ ] Marketing and branding
- [ ] Experiences of all stakeholders
- [ ] Impacts and evaluation
- [ ] Resources
- [ ] Staffing and volunteers

4.1 Introduction

Figure 4.1 illustrates the major management functions to which stakeholder theory and management strategies can be applied. In fact, stakeholders can influence, and be influenced by, ALL aspects of planned events, so this is merely a starting point. Subsequent sub-sections with diagrams look more closely at each of these functional areas and how they influence planned events.

From the theoretical discussions presented so far in this book it should be clear that stakeholders are to be considered an integral part of event management and event tourism, not an isolated issue to be considered once in a while. This suggests that external stakeholder relations be a management function on its own, or tied to a position called something like 'External Relations'. For internal stakeholders a different approach might be required, as each manager within the organization is going to have specific stakeholder issues to deal with on a continuous basis. Bringing these issues into one integrated approach will be the responsibility of the executive.

This chapter also brings other theoretical perspectives to bear on stakeholder management. For example, starting with organizing and planning, we identify five themes for special consideration, each being informed by other theories. Strategies and projects links with institutional theory (e.g., how to become a permanent institution) and project networks including the political market square. Accordingly, these discussions provide a launching point integrating many theoretical perspectives on management.

4.2 Key terms defined

Convention and visitor bureau

A member organization that helps and promote tourism, meetings and business for their areas or cities. In most areas the word Destination Marketing Organization (DMO) is now being used (Fenich, 2013).

Destination marketing/management organizations (DMO)

DMO's are destination marketers, and sometimes they manage event portfolios. They work with members and external stakeholders such as events within the destination to promote it as an attractive place in which to work or invest and that is worth visiting. Events are often viewed by DMOs as a way to enhance the image of the destination, attract tourists, and be catalysts for infrastructure and venue development (Wang & Pizam, 2011; Getz, 2013).

Destination management company (DMC)

"A destination management company, also commonly referred to as a DMC, is a third-party firm that is commonly hired to provide professional services for the planning and implementation of out-of-town event programs and services" Hard, 2018). These services can include program design, logistics management, supplier management and accounting (Hard, 2018).

Political market square

A political perspective, in the analysis of relational interaction in a project network marketing an event, has led to the introduction of a metaphor for such a network, the Political Market Square (Larson, 1997, 2000; Larson & Wikström, 2001).

Public Good Argument

"The key to this powerful argument is to demonstrate important benefits from events and facilities that accrue to society as a whole- or to the economy (which should clearly benefit us all), and to the environment (everyone supports a healthier, safer, more sustainable environment)" Getz (2013).

4.3 Case study - Lusofonia Festival, Macao SAR, China

Ubaldino Sequeira Couto – Institute for Tourism Studies – Macao

Background

The Lusofonia Festival celebrates the diaspora of the Portuguese-speaking communities in Macao, China. It has been celebrated for over 20 years and it was organized by the government to commemorate and recognize the contribution of the Portuguese-speaking communities to Macao's economic and social developments. Following the transfer of sovereignty from Portugal to China in 1999, many from the Portuguese-speaking communities chose to continue to live in Macao and continued playing an important role in Macao's society. These communities are Angola, Brazil, Cape Verde, Guinea-Bissau, collectively Goa, Daman and Diu, Mozambique, São Tomé and Príncipe, East Timor, Portugal and Macao.

Over the course of three days, the festival attracts approximately 30,000 visitors made up of local citizens and tourists. Essentially a cultural festival, the Lusofonia Festival is reminiscent to Portuguese 'festa' events, which are outdoor fairs incorporating food, music, dance and games. Indeed, the major highlight of the Lusofonia Festival is the remarkable booths each representing a Portuguese-speaking community in Macao. These booths introduce to visitors their unique photographs, arts and crafts, costumes, literature, food and wine, most of which influenced by the Portuguese culture reflecting subtle and significant aspects of the Lusophone empire.

Photo 4.1: Lusofonia Festival. Source: Ubaldino Sequeira Couto

The Portuguese-speaking community is an important component to the success of the Lusofonia Festival. It plays various roles as stakeholders but most significantly, the role of both hosts and participants. This case study explores the benefits of engaging the diaspora community that represents different stakeholder groups and sheds light on their role in ensuring the success of the Lusofonia Festival. The observations made in this case study was collected in a wider study by the author exploring the role of diaspora festivals in Macao.

Stakeholders as an integral component in the festival

The diaspora community as a stakeholder group must not be alienated as it is an integral component within the festival organization. The objective of the festival is to commemorate and recognize the contribution of the Portuguese-speaking communities in Macao. It is important that these groups are visibly involved throughout the festival assuming different roles. In addition, the direction bestowed upon Macao by Beijing is to adopt a 'One Centre, One Platform' economic strategy within the Guangdong-Hong Kong-Macao Greater Bay Area and China's Belt and Road Initiative. 'One Centre' refers to the creation of Macao as a World Centre of Tourism and Leisure whereas 'One Platform' refers to the economic and cultural platform between China and Portuguese-speaking countries. Not only the festival fulfills the objective of recognizing the Portuguese-speaking communities but politically, it reiterates their continued contribution to Macao and even at a national level.

Photo 4.2: Lusofonia Festival. Source: Ubaldino Sequeira Couto

Unlike other cultural celebrations and festivals in Macao, the Lusofonia Festival extends beyond a Portuguese theme, but the cultural elements from Portuguese and Portuguese-speaking are diversified, rich and profound. These are manifested in arts and cultural objects, and the involvement of the people from these cultures enriches the authentic experience of festival participants and a realistic Portuguese presence within the society. Although there are a number of Portuguese architectures scattered throughout Macao – a number of these were enlisted as a UNESCO World Heritage Site in 2005 – the Portuguese elements in the city are steadily diminishing. This is in part due to the population characteristics of Macao: first, there was a huge increase of immigrants in the last 20 years following Macao's unprecedented economic boom due to the liberalization of the gaming legislations; second, the majority of the population is ethnically Chinese, diluting the once rich Portuguese and mixed communities in Macao. To put this in a clearer perspective, the population of Macao in 2016 was 650,000, of whom just 40% of the population was born in Macao, and about 1.8% of the total population was ethnically Portuguese or mixed. The Lusofonia Festival contextualize the Portuguese heritage in Macao by offering visitors – local citizens and tourists alike – a close encounter with the Portuguese-speaking communities to experience and learn about their cultures.

Stakeholders must find aesthetic value in the festival

Unlike in a commercial environment, where profitably is a primary concern and stakeholder needs are more apparent, the expectations of the diaspora communities in the Lusofonia Festival are subtle and often less obvious. In order to engage these communities, who are integral to the success of the festival, it is crucial to ensure their needs and expectations are fulfilled. To the majority in the Portuguese-speaking communities, two aesthetic qualities of the Lusofonia Festival are essential to the festival spirit.

The diaspora communities need to feel they belong to the Lusofonia Festival not only as facilitators – as actors in a festival – but be part of it. They look for a good time to enjoy with family and friends, to rekindle with old friends and to meet new acquaintances over food and drinks. For example, many would meet people at the Brazil booth over a glass of *caipirinha*, a very popular Brazilian cocktail. As the Portuguese-speaking countries all share some common cultural traits, for example, in food, many would meet and discuss recipes and special ingredients added to *feijoada*, a traditional Portuguese dish of meat stew with beans, to reflect their country's unique flavor. The diaspora community needs to own the festival in order to be truly part of it. This is evident in their commitment to the festival. For instance, some would spend more than subsidized in order to provide a richer experience to visitors. It was also observed that the majority of the booths representing the countries were decorated by hand, and in some cases, the set-up took days to complete. To ensure the designs reflect an authentic aspect of the culture, members of the diaspora communities personally decorated the booths, often in the evenings after their own full-time work.

The other aesthetic value that the diaspora communities find at the Lusofonia Festival is an opportunity to liminal experience. The work environment – and life – is very different to either of the home cultures. The Lusofonia Festival is reminiscent to Portuguese outdoor festivals, a nostalgic sentiment many in the communities long for. Additionally, the festive atmosphere and physical settings of the festival also remove the barrier that otherwise exists between members of the Portuguese-speaking communities and the general population. Cultural differences, such as language, as well as background like education and employment, almost naturally separate these groups. For instance, the local-born, younger generations of the diaspora communities opt for education in the Portuguese School whereas the majority of the population attends Chinese- or English-medium school. In fact, postcolonial issues often create barriers between members of the Portuguese-speaking communities; the Lusofonia Festival offers a platform for mutual understanding and respect, as well as an opportunity to learn more about each other. This would have been otherwise impossible in usual work, school or social setting.

Stakeholders engage only in supportive environments

Stakeholders' engagement is more profound in a supportive environment. The Lusofonia Festival is an inclusive event; it welcomes and caters for all types of festival goers. Although Portuguese is the predominant language used in the festival, Chinese and English announcements and notices supplement the main commentaries in Portuguese. The majority of the diaspora communities speak Portuguese, Chinese and English which ensure most of the festival visitors are addressed. The festival program also subtly influences the mix of visitors; for instance, children activities like pony riding, face painting, body tattoos and kid games are scheduled in the early afternoon and live bands in the evenings to attract families and adult crowds respectively. In addition, many activities available at the festival encourage participation, for example, sandbag races, foosball tournaments and dances welcome all to join. Parades at the Lusofonia Festival make up of local and international dance troupes from the Portuguese-speaking communities also instill a festive and inclusive atmosphere – such as by physically 'dragging' onlookers into the parade.

Photo 4.3: Lusofonia Festival. Source: Ubaldino Sequeira Couto

The physical environment of the Lusofonia Festival also plays a huge role in engaging stakeholders. The event is held in one of the Portuguese neighborhoods in Macao, with traditional Portuguese houses and buildings, a church and quaint, quiet gardens, along cobblestone roads and pavements. The decorations at the festival as well as booths and crowds instill a festive and joyous mood. Members of the Portuguese-speaking communities are attached to the surroundings and feel like hosts welcoming others to their 'home'. It is usual to see festival goers from the diaspora communities introducing and actively engaged with visitors at the Lusofonia Festival, assuming the role of the host even though they are not staff.

Diaspora communities as a stakeholder group such as the case of Lusofonia Festival in Macao are more involved under certain circumstances, namely,when the stakeholders feel that they are integral to the festival, they find value in it and are engaged in a supportive environment. Although these observations may not apply in other festive events and celebrations, it is prudent that policymakers encourage the continuity of diaspora festivals by providing adequate support, particularly when the organizers and those involved are commonly disadvantaged due to their minority status and access to resources. Diaspora communities, and by extension, ethnic minority groups within a society are essential to the economic and social development of a place; these events are not merely another item to enrich the destination's tourism portfolio.

4.4 Application of management functions to event management

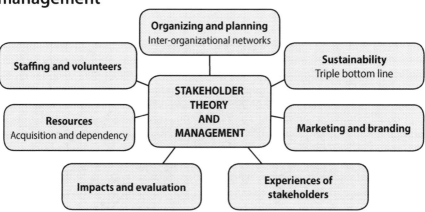

Figure 4.1: Areas of application to event management

4.4.1 Organizing and planning

The very mandate and structure of events and tourism organizations is often set by stakeholders through collaborative efforts. Destination marketing organizations (DMOs), destination management companies (DMC) and convention and visitor bureaus (CVB) are typically viewed as partnerships, bringing together local government, tourism attractions and services, the hotel and hospitality sectors, restaurants and eateries and, of course, events. Many event organizations are completely or partially dependent upon their partnerships with the same organizations as DMOs, DMCs and CVBs and might actually be conceived as collaborations rather than as independent bodies. The literature provides many examples of how festivals and events are organized among partners and through networking (Figure 4.2).

Figure 4.2: Organizing and planning

Strategy and projects

A project network is a graph that an event organizer can use to indicate the sequences in which the essential parts of the event should take place. It can also indicate the dependencies of each part of the event. It should be drawn from the left to the right to indicate the chronology of the elements and when it should take place. Inter-organizational networks can be seen when a group of autonomous stakeholders engage in an interactive process (IBM Center for the Business of Government, 2018). For the event planner it means that multiple stakeholder engages with each other by sharing their goals, norms, rules and structures. By using this strategy of working together, sharing information, activities and resources the event planner can achieve outcomes that they could not have achieved on their own. Scott (2004) looks at institutional theory as the way in which the event planner considers the rules, routines, norms and structures as authoritative guidelines for social behavior.

Organizational culture and change

The culture of the organization will influence the behaviors and values that contribute to its psychological and social environment. Event planners need to understand the ownership of the organization as well as all the shareholders' values and behaviors as this will influence decision-making. This will also determine the resistance to change and the acceptance or rejection of innovative ideas. Understand the history of the organization, communication practices, attitudes and assumptions, as it will assist the event planner to be successful.

Decision making and evaluation

Who is making the decisions in the organization? Who has the authority and control? When organizing and planning an event this is very important to know and understand, as without the necessary permission the event organizer cannot plan a successful event. The event planner needs to understand the complex nature of different systems in science, nature and society and how they interlink with each other. The event planner can also look at different sociological oriented research program on organizations, organizational ecology, and compare rates of failure, change or growth (Smelser & Baltes, 2001).

Community based

The local community plays a very important role in destination events as they provide the social license to operate in the community for the event organizer. It is important to understand that events should adhere to the 'public good' argument. Organizers must involve the community in the event planning process and see it as a very important stakeholder. They must also protect the interest and needs of the community and ensure that benefits will come from the event.

Collaboration

Events have different stakeholders all with their own individual interest but collaborative relationships (collaboration theory) need to be established by the event organizer to perform the project task. Understanding political processes in the event project network will assist the event organizer to manage either consensus or conflict between these stakeholders (Larson & Wikström, 2001). Stakeholders also have different power and legitimacy to influence the planning and organizing phase according to Savage et al. (1991) as earlier discussed, and this needs to be taken into consideration. The processes and methods used to facilitate the peaceful ending of conflict is defined as conflict resolution (Grimble & Wellard, 1997). Value can be created as different stakeholders work together towards the greater good of all (Prebensen, 2010). Spiropoulos, Gargalianos and Sotiriadou (2005) acknowledge that the strategic planning process and stakeholder management is seen as a crucial component for producing successful events.

Research notes

Prebensen, N. (2010). Value creation through stakeholder participation: A case study of an event in The High North. *Event Management*, **14** (1), 37-52.

Abstract: Value creation as a result of stakeholders' participation and involvement is explored in network and co-creation frameworks. The study analyzes seven various stakeholder groups and their purposes for, and structures in, joining an event in the High North. In addition, the study examines the stakeholders' evaluation of values created through their own and others' participation in the event (i.e., value co-creation). The case study is a dog-sled race in Finnmark,

Norway, the Finnmarksløpet. The stakeholders include both organizations and individuals. The study employs various explorative techniques to acknowledge value creation within a stakeholder perspective. The findings reveal that the various groups entail numerous reasons for participating in the event, classified as autotelic and instrumental value experiences. The stakeholders experience various types of values through their participation and involvement, dependent of their own—or in the case of representing a firm, the firm's—motivation and participation in the event. The study explores value creation as a consequence of other stakeholders' participation as well; that is, the sponsors get amplified value with increased media coverage, and more spectators' participation (by their presence or via various mediums). As a result, the event becomes more attractive for both sponsors and media. The host organization receives value from all stakeholders' participations. The study also points to how destinations might gain values through networking and cooperation, exemplified by stakeholders' involvement and participation in an event.

Keywords: co-creation; experience; networks; stakeholder; values

Spiropoulos, S., Gargalianos, D., & Sotiriadou, K. (2005). The 20th Greek festival of Sydney: a stakeholder analysis. *Event Management*, 9(4), 169-183.

Abstract: In response to the demand for the adoption of a corporate culture by not-for-profit festivals, festival organizations increasingly identify strategic planning process and stakeholder management as crucial components for successful events. The purpose of this article is to present a framework developed for categorizing ethnic festivals stakeholders from a functional role (i.e., marketing, administration, and production) and an ethnic origin (i.e., Greek, Greek-Australian, and non-Greek) perspective. The proposed framework was developed and applied to the 20th Greek Festival of Sydney (GFS), which was held in 2002, by identifying, categorizing, and examining the role of its stakeholders in the management and delivery of the event. The identification of the type of stakeholders, the ways they influence the GFS organization, and the strategic implications that derived from their involvement are addressed. The methodology utilized to develop the stakeholder framework was qualitative in nature. It combined triangulated data that derived from a number of interviews with representatives from the GFS administration, participant observations, and content analysis of internal documents and reports. The GFS stakeholder analysis offered an understanding of the several marketing- administration- and production-related strategic implications to the organization and running of the festival, such as the impact on its content, participants, and future development. The proposed framework derives from the GFS case study, yet it has the potential to be used for the examination of stakeholders' strategic implications to other ethnic festivals.

Keywords: Ethnic festivals; event stakeholder; stakeholder functions; strategic planning

4.4.2 Sustainability

This area concerns more than the greening of events; it covers their long-term viability. Risk needs to be determined across all networks as well as stakeholder influences on the event portfolio of the area. The overall health of the events in an area (i.e., the population of events) needs to be investigated as well as their dependency upon the resources of the area (Figure 4.3). Karlsen & Nordström (2009) indicate that if the festival cooperates with multiple stakeholders who work together as global networks, the event can be more sustainable. Another aspect that is important for sustainability was identified by the study of Presbury & Edwards (2005). They found that it is important to incorporate sustainability objectives into meetings and event management planning. In their research of 'Utilizing the VICE model for the sustainable development of the Innibos Arts Festival', van Niekerk & Coetzee (2011, 347) indicate that for an event to be sustainable you need to: *"balance the needs and demands of the visitors to the festival, the tourism industry as a whole, and the surrounding community with a focus on the environment."*

Risk

Hosting an event opens the event organizer up to potential risks. Leopkey and Parent (2009) in their study write that risk management is a proactive process that should strategically identify, anticipate, prevent, minimize and mitigate all possible risks to the stakeholdes in an event. It is important to manage the risks because failing to recognize the potential problems might have huge impacts on your organization. The sustainability of events can increase if the risk that threatens the event can be shared across networks. During the planning and organizing phase, shared risk should be incorporated. This can include financial loss, damage to facilities, loss of equipment and reputation, injury of employees, volunteers or participants, security and food safety concerns to mention a few.

Legitimacy

Various stakeholders are present when planning and organizing events. These stakeholders are driven by their own needs and reasons for being involved in the event. Event planners should determine the legitimacy of each stakeholder and plan in advance how they will be managed. Their legitimacy will also be determined by the political market square and the social behavior acceptable during the negotiated exchanges. According to Getz & Andersson (2008: p.13) events become institutions when: *"sufficient support and resources are assured by key external stakeholders, leading to a taken-for-granted permanence, and premised on the festival solving important social problems (or meeting important social goals). This is the 'niche' required by population ecology and resource dependency theory, and presumably a niche cannot be occupied simultaneously by more than one institution".*

Resources

Dependency of resources occur at an interorganizational relationship level if the one organization has a need for a resource and the other organization has control over that resource (Pfeffer & Salancik, 1978).

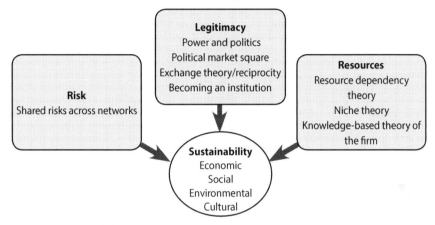

Figure 4.3: Sustainability

Research notes

Getz, D., & Andersson, T. D. (2008). Sustainable festivals: On becoming an institution. *Event Management*, **12**(1), 1-17.

Abstract: This article conceptually addresses the sustainability of festivals from the perspective of the organizations providing them, especially in the context of how event organizations can become permanent institutions. Festivals and other recurring events are often viewed as tourist attractions, and are commonly used in place marketing and destination image-making strategies. Little attention has been paid, however, to their individual or collective viability and long-term sustainability. Supportive data are provided from a survey of 14 live-music festivals in Sweden in which responding festival managers confirmed the importance of attaining 'institutional status', occupying a unique 'niche' in the community, sustaining committed stakeholders, and practicing constant innovation. Theoretical conclusions are drawn on the institutionalization process for festivals, including a set of propositions that can be used both as indicators of institutional status, and as hypotheses for future research.

Keywords: Sustainability; festivals; event organizations; stakeholders; institutions

Karlsen, S., & Stenbacka Nordström, C. (2009). Festivals in the Barents Region: Exploring festival-stakeholder cooperation. *Scandinavian Journal of Hospitality and Tourism*, **9**(2-3), 130-145.

Abstract: The paper reports from a multiple case study investigating three music festivals located in the Barents region, namely the *Festspel i Pite Älvdal* (Piteå,

Sweden), the *Festspillene i Nord-Norge* (Harstad, Norway) and the *Jutajaiset Folk-lorefestivaali* (Rovaniemi, Finland). The aim of the reported study was to investigate how these festivals cooperated with actors in their surroundings. Furthermore, the purpose was to explore the study's data through the perspectives of network and stakeholder theory. The data consisted of field notes from observations of 58 festival events; 10 in-depth interviews with festival administrators and official representatives of the festivals' host municipalities; and documentation. The data was analyzed using meaning condensation and structuring displays. Through the theory-related exploration of the study's data, three themes emerged: first, the festivals cooperated with multiple stakeholders, who assumed multiple roles; second, the festivals and their stakeholders would sometimes enter into a state of symbiosis; and third, the festivals were seen to engage in long-stretched, 'loose' and global networks. The three themes appeared as interrelated and could all be understood as strategies, which the festivals employed in order to increase their sustainability. The findings could also be connected to a typology of festivals in the context of institutionalization.

Keywords: Festival research, festival-stakeholder cooperation, festival management, network theory, stakeholder theory

Presbury, R. & Edwards, D. C. (2005). Incorporating sustainability in meetings and event management education. *International Journal of Event Management Research*, **1**(1) 30-45.

Abstract: Events and other meetings are an important component of the tourism industry. The activities around events and other meetings bring people together and offer communities an opportunity to celebrate and showcase their traditions, culture and way of life. As the major stakeholders in such activities realize the significant economic benefits of holding events and meetings, governments and operators are making significant capital investment in developing the necessary facilities and infrastructure to accommodate this sector of the tourism industry. Whilst the flurry of activities has a number of positive economic impacts, such as job creation and increased revenue there are also potential negative consequences. The quality of the economic, social and natural environments in which such activity takes place is at risk. As a result, there has been a realization, particularly by educators and researchers that there is a need to incorporate sustainability into meeting and event management. The Best Education Network (BEST) has addressed this gap by holding workshops for the purpose of identifying objectives that can be used in the development of a short teaching module for sustainable meeting and event management. The purpose of this paper is to discuss the need to incorporate sustainability into meeting and event management; to describe the process used by BEST to identify sustainable meeting and event objectives; and to present the learning objectives that were identified, as a result of this process.

Keywords: Sustainability, meetings, event

Van Niekerk, M., & Coetzee, W. J. L. (2011). Utilizing the VICE model for the sustainable development of the Innibos Ar ts Festival. *Journal of Hospitality Marketing & Management*, **20**(3-4), 347-365.

Abstract: The purpose of the study is to ensure the continuous and sustainable growth of the Innibos Arts Festival in South Africa while balancing the needs and demands of the visitors to the festival, the tourism industry as a whole, and the surrounding community with a focus on the environment. Continuous growth of festivals in South Africa is ensured as government supports and promotes this as part of its strategy for economic development. However, the sustainability of the festivals has come under scrutiny as many of these festivals compete for similar tourism markets. Destination managers and developers all over the world, but specifically in New Zealand and the United Kingdom, have identified the visitors, industry, community, and environment (VICE) model as a critical success factor in the sustainable development of any tourism destination. Equitable interaction among the VICE must occur before the tourism destination will be sustainable. The VICE model was used to identify the profiles, demands, and needs of the visitors to the festival; the role and impact of the event on the industry and businesses; the impact on the Nelspruit community and environment (where the Innibos Arts Festival is held); and how these elements should synergize with a view to ensure sustainability. Self-completion questionnaires were used to determine the sustainability of the festival. A total of 2,584 visitor surveys, 206 business surveys, and 520 community surveys, which included questions on the environmental concept, were completed over the past 5 years (2004–2008). The results of the study indicated that the VICE model was successfully utilized in the study of the Innibos Arts Festival. It highlighted critical areas in the different categories of the VICE model that require attention and development. The successful management and development of these critical aspects would ensure the sustainability of the festival. It can therefore be concluded that the VICE model can be utilized to ensure the sustainability of festivals.

Keywords: VICE model, sustainable development, arts festival

Leopkey, B. & Parent, M. M. (2009). Risk management issues in large-scale sporting events: A stakeholder perspective. *European Sport Management Quarterly*, **9**(2), 187-208.

Abstract: The purpose of this paper is to identify the risk management issues in large-scale sporting events from the perspective of the organizing committee members and stakeholders. A comparative case study analysis of two major Canadian sporting events (the International Skating Union 2006 World Figure Skating Championships and the U-20 Fédération Internationale de Football Association World Cup Canada 2007) was conducted through analysis of archival material and interviews. A revised definition of risk management emerged from the data: "risk management is a proactive process that involves assessing all possible risks to the events and its stakeholders by strategically anticipating, preventing, minimizing, and planning responses to mitigate those identified risks". Fifteen risk issue categories were also identified by the various stakeholder groups. The categories were: environment, financial, human resources, infrastructure, interdependence, legacy, media, operations, organizing, participation, political, relationships, sport, threats, and visibility.

Keywords: international marathon; large scale sport events; risk management; stakeholder.

4.4.3 Marketing and branding

Marketing is first and foremost aimed at the guest or customer, always a key stakeholder, but there is also internal marketing to consider (staff and volunteers) and exchange relationships with sponsors, suppliers, grant givers and any other influential groups (Figure 4.4).

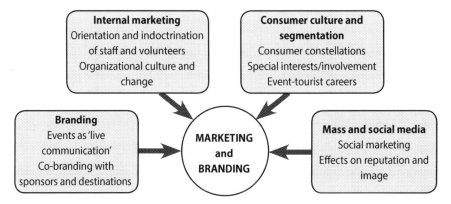

Figure 4.4: Marketing and branding

Branding

DMOs are established primarily to sell and to promote the destination as well as to assist the members of their organizations in their marketing efforts. They develop branding strategies for whole destinations, and this can involve co-branding with events that help establish or reinforce the destination brand. Most important are the images conveyed by events, and the brand values they help express, such as "inviting, friendly, safe, diverse, or attractive all year round." Co-branding is the effort of two or more partners to associate their individual brands for mutual gains. Mossberg & Getz (2006) revealed in their research that many festivals would co-brand with their city and sponsors. They also looked at how festival branding is influenced by brand ownership in a multi-stakeholder environment.

Some branding strategies are highly targeted at special interest groups, such as amateur athletes or food lovers, in which case particular 'iconic' events can form important strategic elements. From a corporate point of view, a company brand can be brought to life through inspired and innovative design and experiences, with events being conceived as live communications.

Internal marketing

When planning events, it is important that the organizers understand the orientation and indoctrination of the staff and volunteers. Their buy-in to the event's mandate and culture should be obtained through internal marketing. This involves an understanding of organizational culture, encompassing the beliefs, assumptions, values and ways of interaction that have been established. Changing organizational culture can be very difficult, especially when founders are sustaining their leadership. Conflicts can arise when profound changes in culture or strategy are suggested. Organizational culture has been a major theme in the management literature and a great deal of advice is available. (See, for example: Schein, 1992; Free Management Library, http://managementhelp.org/organizations/culture.htm.)

Consumer culture and segmentation

With customers being a critical stakeholder group, knowledge of their consumption culture(s), and an ability to segment target markets accordingly, is essential. Many people will travel for special interests, some at a high level of involvement and commitment to their leisure and lifestyle pursuits, and event organizers must be familiar with their preferences. Research by Tkaczynski (2013) is a good example of how a music festival used attendee segmentation to find similarities in characteristics and behavioral patterns between groups.

'Consumption constellations' are defined as *"clusters of complementary products, specific brands and/or consumption activities used by consumers to define, communicate and enact social roles"* (Solomon & Buchanan 1991, p. 191). Events that provide similar benefits, such as physical challenges for amateur athletes, can therefore be marketed as a package. Research on 'event travel careers' has revealed how motivation, travel patterns, destinations and event choices evolve with increasing involvement in sports, lifestyle and leisure pursuits (e.g., Getz and Andersson, 2010; Getz and McConnell, 2011 & 2014) and this theory provides insights to better marketing.

Mass and social media

The event organizer of today should work with an array of alternative social marketing methods. Bloggers, e-zines, websites, Facebook, Twitter and Snapchat can all be used to market the event to potential attendees. Event organizers should understand how specific groups view a destination, as well as the effects of an event on the reputation and image of the destination. Stakeholders can assist with mass and social media and so ensure the sustainability of the event. The local and national media can also play a very important role in the public perception of the socio-cultural effects of festivals as indicated in the study of Robertson & Rogers (2009).

Research notes

Mossberg, L., & Getz, D. (2006). Stakeholder influences on the ownership and management of festival brands. *Scandinavian Journal of Hospitality and Tourism*, 6(4), 308-326.

Abstract: The purpose of this paper is to investigate how brand ownership in a multi-stakeholder environment influences festival branding. Through 14 case studies, it was revealed that many festivals co-brand through incorporation of city, geographical or sponsor names in the festival name. In Sweden, stakeholder involvement in the branding process was uniformly low, while in the Calgary festivals in Canada it ranged from low to high. As well, ownership of the brand was controlled singly by the Swedish festival organizations, while in Calgary most brands were diffusely owned through sponsors' involvement. Areas for further research on festival branding are suggested, including the need to further explore brand ownership and control within a stakeholder context.

Keywords: Festivals, brand ownership, brand management, stakeholders, Canada, Sweden

Tkaczynski, A. (2013). A stakeholder approach to attendee segmentation: A case study of an Australian Christian music festival. *Event Management*, 17 (3), 283-298.

Abstract: Festivals provide many benefits to regions and communities such as tourism expenditure, community pride, and the celebration of culture. Whereas the literature has emphasized the need to incorporate stakeholders into the management of festivals, researchers have not considered how these stakeholders are segmenting their attendees. This article applies a stakeholder approach to attendee segmentation through a case study with semistructured interviews to profile visitors to Easterfest, an Australian Christian music festival. The results suggest that stakeholders, although not actively segmenting visitors, share many similarities in their description of the characteristics and behavioral patterns of attendees to the festival. Limitations based on the findings are made while future opportunities are also outlined.

Keywords: Easterfest, festival, market segmentation, stakeholder theory

Robertson, M., & Rogers, P. (2009). Festivals, cooperative stakeholders and the role of the media: A case analysis of newspaper media. *Scandinavian Journal of Hospitality and Tourism*, 9(2-3), 206-224.

Abstract: Image, brand narrative and stakeholder collaboration each represent pivotal paradigms in the analysis, evaluation and formation of good management practice for festivals. The role of the media as significant intermediary offers a core measurement instrument linking these paradigms. This exploratory work applies a two-stage empirical study to investigate and posit a methodological procedure for this instrument. A principal component analysis of data relating to the scales of significance given by festival visitors and festival directors, respectively, to the socio-cultural effects of festivals indicates that both the local media and national media are strong elements in the emerging factors. A further media framing methodology is provided to assess variations in the role of newspapers (a medium identified as particularly significant in the decision making process of festival goers) in converging agendas which may influence and vary the public perception of the socio-cultural influences of festivals. The authors conclude that these agendas are affiliated and can be measured with reference to the factors that emerged in the principal component analysis.

Keywords: Festivals, attendees and directors, rural and urban, media framing, stakeholders

4.4.4 Experiences of stakeholders

It is not just the customer experience that matters; each stakeholder has an experience associated with the event (whether they attend or not) and each stakeholder attaches meanings to the event (Figure 4.5).

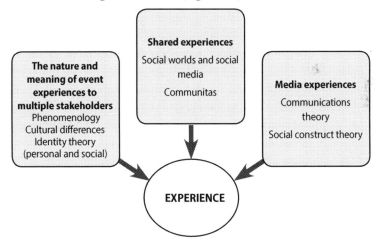

Figure 4.5: Experience

The nature and meaning of event experiences to multiple stakeholders

Stakeholders will have different experiences before, during and after events (Buch, Milne and Dickson, 2011). These differences can be studied through 'phenomenology', being a methodology to study the nature and structure of an experience while it is taking place (Beard and Russ, 2017). Culture, related to belief systems and traditions, will also play a role in how stakeholders differently experience events. Identity theory, concerning how both personal and social identity is formed and how it influences behavior, is another possible foundation to the study of event experiences (Benkendorff & Pearce, 2012).

Table 4.1, adapted and simplified from Getz and Page (*Event Studies*, 3rd ed., 2016, pp. 246-7) can assist the event organizer to identify multiple stakeholders and the unique or most important elements of their event experiences. Of course, they should be asked! Many of these stakeholders have a particular stake in the success of the event, or a responsibility for its production, but might also want to enjoy some aspects of the overall experience.

Table 4.1: The experiences of different stakeholders

General categories of stakeholders having event experiences	Unique or especially important experiential dimensions (not mutually exclusive)
Paying customers; spectators Invited guests The public at free events Event tourists	Generic benefits: escape, being entertained, socializing, quality time with family and friends
	Targeted benefits: seeking specific attributes of the event and destination, such as the food, or the entertainers, or authentic cultural experiences; learning
	Communitas: belonging and sharing, or sub-culture engagement
	Identity building/reinforcement; being part of a group, however temporary; their experiences can be extended through social media
	Emotionally involved, loyal fans also experience nostalgia
Athletic participants in sport events	High involvement leads to an event travel career including multiple events that provide desired benefits such as meeting challenges, athletic development, personal growth, self esteem
Elite athletes in competitions	Elite athletes might stress personal improvement, winning, prize money, career advancement, adulation of fans
Producers and organizers Owners; investors	First and foremost they want a successful event; might feel stress
Media personnel	Organizers have to ensure the media get the coverage and stories they want, and enjoy their entire experience
Media audiences (not live spectators)	Being entertained, informed Feeling part of a fan 'family'
Staff	Professional conduct and responsibility defines their main involvement, but enjoyment of the event can also be important
Volunteers	Volunteers often have specific interests in the event theme or program; communitas among volunteers and staff can be important
	The 'cast' is part of the experience for others; service providers can be as important as the quality of the program in shaping others' experiences
Performers at events and in arts competitions	They want to excel and be appreciated; learn from others; perhaps winning is important for some

Officials Representatives of governing bodies	Must first and foremost fulfill their responsibilities, then try to enjoy the event
Sponsors and grant givers VIPs (celebrities, politicians, etc.)	Sponsors often act as hosts, responsible for the enjoyment of their invitees VIPs are generally given special treatment, and might expect something extra special
Suppliers and vendors Exhibitors	They will have contractual obligations to fulfill They need to generate sales, marketing leads and contacts, and so have to put work ahead of enjoyment
Exhibition and conference attendees	Socializing/networking might be as important as learning Event producers/owners want to measure return on experience, meaning how much the experience affects the attendee leading to improved ROI, loyalty, etc.
Regulators: police, fire, health inspectors, etc.	Must fulfill their duties, keep people safe, and contribute to the enjoyment of others
The public not directly involved in the event)	The public's experience can range from 'psychic benefits' such as pride, to being inconvenienced or harmed by traffic, or amenity loss like noise

Shared experiences

Social worlds and social media are increasingly important in disseminating information and in reaching stakeholders. Social networking is successful when you have clear-targeted stakeholders and know how to reach them. Many people share their positive or negative experiences of the event on social media. When planning and organizing an event it is important for the organizers to keep the social world in mind and facilitate communication through it. *"Communitas is a vehicle for focusing event-goers and other stakeholders' attention on targeted social issues, meaning the event becomes a social marketing tool"* (Getz, 2013: 144).

Media experiences

S.F. Scudder proposed the communications theory in the 1980s; it states that all living entities communicate, but the way they communicate differs (Scudder, 1980). The media will communicate their event experiences in different ways and different people will have different experiences at the same event. Social construct theory helps us to structure our experience and analysis of the world into categories. When planning and organizing an event the organizer needs to keep this in mind, and think how the media will communicate, categorize and disseminate their experiences.

Research note

Buch, T., Milne, S. & Dickson, G. (2011). Multiple stakeholder perspectives on cultural events: Auckland's Pasifika Festival. *Journal of Hospitality Marketing & Management*, **20**(3-4), 311-328.

Abstract: Cultural festivals can assist local communities in showcasing cultural attributes and can offer the chance to strengthen a sense of identity. The Pasifika Festival, held annually in Auckland, New Zealand, is a celebration of the city's Pacific Island communities. Drawing on audience and stallholder surveys, and interviews/meetings with festival organizers, this article provides a multiple stakeholder perspective on the festival experience and what it means to those who are part of it. The article also addresses the important question of how to conduct robust, cost-effective research in large festival settings, focusing on the use of online survey tools.

Keywords: Cultural festivals, stakeholders, Pacific Island communities, Auckland, online research

4.4.5 Impacts and evaluation

Managers have to evaluate all their operations for effectiveness – that is, to ensure the event is produced as intended and with the desired outcomes (Long, 2000). They also have to continuously evaluate efficiency, how well the event obtains and uses resources. But external stakeholders are also evaluating the event from their perspectives (Figure 4.6). Many studies investigate the socio-cultural, economic and environmental impacts of events on the area (Jackson, 2008).

For details on event evaluation and impact assessment, including stakeholder involvement, see these two companion books:

Getz, D. (2018). *Event Evaluation: Theory and Methods for Event Management and Tourism*. Oxford: Goodfellow Publishers.

Getz, D. (2018). *Event Impact Assessment: Theory and Methods for Event Management and Tourism*. Oxford: Goodfellow Publishers.

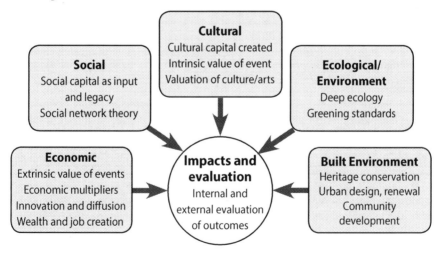

Figure 4.6: Impacts and evaluation

Research note

Jackson, L. A. (2008). Residents' perceptions of the impacts of special event tourism. *Journal of Place Management and Development*, **1**(3), 240-255.

Abstract: *Purpose*: The purpose of this research was to explore residents' perceptions of special event tourism at a destination. Specifically, the research examined residents' perceptions of the social, economic and environmental impacts of special event tourism on the destination. The study also examined dimensions of community life that were impacted or curtailed as a result of event tourism.

Design/methodology/approach: Data were collected by means of a telephone survey. The survey solicited residents' perceptions of the social, economic, and environmental impacts of special event tourism. The study was exploratory and followed a descriptive design.

Findings: Residents are generally in favor of events that contribute socially and economically to the destination. They are, however, ambivalent to some of the negative impacts, but are willing to cope with these as long as the perceived benefits exceed the negative impacts.

Research limitations/implications: Although the sample was adequate for statistical analysis, a larger sample size would yield more generalizable results. Consequently, caution should be used in making generalizations based on this study.

Practical implications: The constant question faced by destination managers and tourism development authorities is how to plan for optimal tourism development, while at the same time minimize its impact on the resident population. One approach is to monitor residents' opinions of perceived impacts as a means of incorporating community reaction into tourism planning and development. Hence, this study proposes an all-inclusive community-centric approach to event tourism policy-making rather than a top-down approach.

Originality/value: Both practitioners and educators will benefit from the results of this study as it provides insight into a destination's residents' perceptions of special event tourism. This topic has received little attention in the past.

Keywords: Tourism, tourism development, communities

Economic impacts

When measuring the economic impact of the event, its extrinsic value is important. Economic impacts can be very important for businesses while associations and government might be less interested in its economic impact. Economic multipliers and input-output models are used to calculate the incremental tourist expenditure 'direct, indirect or induced' of the event on the local economy (Curtis et al., 2017). Events are used to bring 'new money' into the destination, which is usually achieved through events in the portfolio that are tourist attractions. Certain events can be very innovative and the dissemination of the economic benefits is important for the community. Events do not create a lot of permanent employment but can however be used in the destination during the low season to smooth out the seasonality curve. Events will therefore assist in creating more permanent jobs throughout the destination. Many scholars have done research on the economic impacts of events in the destination from various stakeholders' point of view.

Research note

Curtis, J., Hynes, S., O'Reilly, P. & Breen, B. (2017). Recreational angling tournaments: Participants' expenditures. *Journal of Sport & Tourism*, **21** (3), 201–221.

Abstract: Fishing tournaments are a common feature in recreational angling across a wide range of target species in both fresh and salt waters. Tournaments are organised for a number of purposes, including as commercial enterprises; as fund-raising initiatives for angling clubs; for economic development purposes (e.g. tourism); as well as improve participants' skill levels. Most tournaments are confined to geographically small areas and usually occur over a small number of days, which can mean a pulse of economically significant activity in the local area. This paper analyses the nature of expenditure associated with angling tournaments, including travel, food and accommodation, and angling-related expenditures as a function of socio-economic and angler characteristics. Analysis based on 106 tournaments across Ireland during 2013 finds a clear 80/20 segmentation between 'high'- and 'low'-spend anglers and that the segmentation occurs across all fish target species considered. The analysis also finds that British coarse anglers participating at Irish angling tournaments spend considerably more than other anglers irrespective of target species or angler country of origin.

Keywords: Expenditure; competitive angling; angler preferences; recreational fishing; tournament fishing.

Social impacts

Not all events need to make money or are organized to make money. In many cases events are organized by the community for the community. Social capital can be used to create value in the long term in the community (Hall & Hodges, 1996). For instance venues are built during events (Liu, 2016) and can be used by the community after the event. Social network theory looks at how different stakeholders will interact with each other inside of their networks. Stakeholders want to see the social impacts of events whether it is promoting local pride or a sense of belonging. Social impacts of events can be both positive and negative.

Research note

Liu, D. (2016). Social impact of major sports events perceived by host community. *International Journal of Sports Marketing and Sponsorship*, **17**(1), 78-91.

Abstract: *Purpose*: The purpose of this paper is to examine the social impact of major sports events perceived by host city residents using Shanghai as an example.

Design/methodology/approach: Exploratory factor analysis based on 450 valid questionnaires.

Findings: Research revealed six impact factors including four positive ones: 'image and status', 'international exchange and cooperation', 'economic and tourism development', and 'infrastructure development'. In addition, two negative ones are also identified as 'inconvenience of life' and 'environment pollution and security concern'. Taken as a whole, the local residents in Shanghai have a relative positive perception of the impact of major sports events. Four out of six impact factors were significantly predictive of the attitude toward future bidding of major sports events.

Originality/value: The existing literature mainly examined social impact of specific events through case study, and little is known about the overall perception of major sports events in general. Accordingly, this paper seeks to bridge the gap by taking an event portfolio approach using Shanghai as an example.

Keywords: Attitude, social impact, major events, residents' perceptions

Hall, C. M., & Hodges, J. (1996). The party's great, but what about the hangover?: The housing and social impacts of mega-events with special reference to the 2000 Sydney Olympics. *Festival Management and Event Tourism*, **4**(1-1), 13-20.

Abstract: Mega-events, such as the Olympic Games and world fairs, are a major factor in tourism development, urban revitalization, and urban reimaging strategies. However, despite their economic, social, and political significance, it is only within the last decade that substantial attention has been paid to their impact and legacies. This article provides a discussion of the scope and definition of mega-events, an analysis of the reasons why mega-events are held, and offers an examination of the housing and social impact of mega-events on host cities and regions with special reference to the housing and social planning of the Sydney 2000 Olympic Games. The article concludes that the focus on the economic dimension of events is often at the expense of social, environmental, and political analyses.

Keywords: Housing impact; mega-event impact; social impact; Sydney 2000 Olympic Games

Cultural impacts

Not all impacts of events are tangible. Cultural capital can be used to organize events, events can create intrinsic value and are valued because of the awareness that it creates about a specific culture. In some instances, events are being used to preserve the culture of the area or to create a renewed interest in it. An example of this can be seen in the article of van Niekerk & Coetzee (2011): *"Hauptfleisch (2006) and Coetser, J. (2002) suggest that the Afrikaans-language festivals started in the 1990s when the Afrikaans-speaking population (6 million out of 44 million people currently in South Africa) began to fear the extinction of their language and culture under the new South African dispensation and its expressed preference for English as the lingua franca"*. Schlenker, Edwards & Sheridan (2005) study develops a framework to assess the socio-cultural impacts of festivals on host communities. Quality of life and wellbeing of the local residents are also two aspects for the continuous support of an event.

Research note

Schlenker, K., Edwards, D. C., & Sheridan, L. (2005). A flexible framework for evaluating the socio-cultural impacts of a small festival. *International Journal of Event Management Research*, 1(1) 66-77.

Abstract: The increasing popularity of festivals and events, coupled with their positive and negative impacts on host communities, has led to a growing body of research on the impacts of festivals and events. As a substantial amount of this research has focused on assessing the economic impacts of festivals, there is growing demand for the measurement of the socio-cultural impacts of these festivals and events. To address this, issue a study was conducted that developed a framework for the social impact evaluation of festivals and piloted a tool that measured the community perceptions of socio-cultural impacts. This paper has four aims. First, it provides an overview of the importance of understanding community perceptions of socio-cultural impacts that may arise from the staging of festivals and events. Second, the paper outlines a Social Impact Evaluation (SIE) framework suitable for the holistic evaluation of socio-cultural impacts of festivals and events. Third the paper reports on the piloting of a tool, the Social Impact Perception (SIP) scale that was created to measure community perceptions of socio-cultural impacts that may arise from the staging of a small community festival. Fourth, the paper provides recommendations for the future application of the SIE framework and the SIP scale.

Keywords: Social impact perception, measurement, events

Environmental/ecological impacts

The environmental impacts of events have been receiving more attention but Collins, Jones & Munday (2009) indicate that it is difficult to assess quantitatively. Some ecological areas, for example islands, can be more environmentally sensitive than others, and event organizers should carefully consider the impacts of the events before choosing them. Human life is important, but just one of many equal components of a global ecosystem, as seen by the deep ecology movement. Greening standards and certifications are been implemented in the event industry, but more focus should be given to this, as well as how local residents perceived their influences on events (Guizzardi, Mariani, & Prayag: 2017).

Research note

Collins, A., Jones, C. & Munday, M. (2009). Assessing the environmental impacts of mega sporting events: Two options? *Tourism Management*, **30**(6), 828-837.

Abstract: At a time when public and private agencies recognize the importance of sustainable development, the environmental impacts of mega sporting events are commanding increasing attention. However, despite event sponsors often flagging the importance of environmental as well as socio-economic legacy components, the environmental impacts of events are difficult to assess quantitatively, being complex and often occurring over extended periods. The general assessment issue is particularly acute with regard to mega events such as the Olympic Games and FIFA World Cup. The practical issues mean that any quantitative techniques seeking to assess environmental impacts are likely to be partial in scope. This paper examines two such approaches for quantitative impact assessment of selected environmental externalities connected with visitation at sporting events. The paper considers the use of Ecological Footprint analysis and Environmental Input–Output modeling. It provides examples of the applications of these techniques to discrete sporting events in a UK region, and discusses whether these techniques are appropriate for exploring the environmental impacts of mega events.

Keywords: Mega events; economic impact; environmental impact; environmental accounting; ecological footprint analysis

Guizzardi, A., Mariani, M., & Prayag, G. (2017). Environmental impacts and certification: evidence from the Milan World Expo 2015. *International Journal of Contemporary Hospitality Management*, **29**(3), 1052-1071.

Abstract: *Purpose*: This study aims to examine residents' perceptions of environmental impacts and certification for the Milan World Expo 2015 as well as their overall attitude toward the mega-event.

Design/methodology/approach: A survey of Milan residents based on a convenience sample led to 221 useable questionnaires.

Findings: Residents perceived that the Expo will have minimal negative and positive environmental impacts. A minority of residents were aware of the environmental certification of the event. The less agreeable residents were with the perceived negative environmental impacts of the event, the more agreeable they were that a certification of event sustainability should limit the damage to the natural environment. Residents' perceptions of the certification were positively related to their overall attitude toward the event.

Research limitations/implications: The findings cannot be generalized to other mega-events but have several managerial implications in relation to the need for information provision to residents and better communication of the certification by event organizers and planners.

Originality/value: Despite rising concerns about environmental issues related to hosting mega-events, there is no research on perceptions of a certification of event sustainability by residents.

Keywords: Environmental impact, mega-event, environmental certification, Expo 2015, residents' attitude

Built environmental impact

Events can be used for heritage conservation in the built environment. Azzali (2017) and Chalkley & Essex (1999) demonstrate that mega-events are used as catalyst for urban development and improve building planning capacity. Azzali (2017) also found that urban design knowledge could be transferred after the event to other cities. Kassens-Noor (2016) writes that although mega-events can be used to transform cities and increase community development it can lead to dystopias and lead to geographically uneven and politically volatile trajectories of urban development (Gotham, 2015).

Research note

Azzali, S. (2017). Mega-events and urban planning: Doha as a case study. *Urban Design International*, **22**(1), 3-12.

Abstract: Hosting mega-events can not only catalyse urban development, but also lead to an improvement of local planning systems and building planning capacity. Events can create knowledge transfer from one city to another, and be used as tools for experimenting new prototypes and urban templates but on a smaller scale. Within this context, this research aims at identifying strategies for leveraging mega-events to improve local planning capacity. Relevant best practices in the use of events as planning enhancers are derived from the literature, and then applied to a case study, the city of Doha. In fact, the capital of Qatar has all the characteristics for benefiting from events. First, it is a city that has already and will host in the imminent future many international events. Second, Doha is managing with difficulties its rapid urban development, and needs to improve its planning system. Results show there is a potential for benefiting from events in two ways: they can assist knowledge transfer from international consultancy to local agencies, and vice versa. In addition, events can act as the glue for overcoming the fragmentation of Doha's planning system, by facilitating the implementation of 2030 Qatar National Vision, the country's comprehensive blueprint.

Keywords: Doha Gulf Region, mega-events, urban policy, urban planning.

Kassens-Noor, E. (2016). From ephemeral planning to permanent urbanism: An urban planning theory of mega-events. *Urban Planning*, **1**(1), 41-54.

Abstract: Mega-events like the Olympic Games are powerful forces that shape cities. In the wake of mega-events, a variety of positive and negative legacies have remained in host cities. In order to bring some theoretical clarity to debates about legacy creation, I introduce the concepts of the mega-event utopia, dystopia and heterotopia. A mega-event utopia is ideal and imaginary urbanism embracing abstract concepts about economies, socio-political systems, spaces, and societies in the host during events. The mega-event utopia (in contrast to other utopian visions other stakeholders may hold) is dictated by the desires of the mega-event owners irrespective of the realities in the event host. In short, a mega-event utopia is the perfect event host from the owner's perspective. Mega-event utopias are suggested as a theoretical model for the systematic transformation of their host cities. As large-scale events progress as ever more powerful transformers into this century, mega-event dystopias have emerged as negatives of these idealistic utopias. As hybrid post-event landscapes, mega-event heterotopias manifest the temporary mega-event utopia as legacy imprints into the long-term realities in hosting cities. Using the Olympic utopia as an example of a mega-event utopia, I theorize utopian visions around four urban traits: economy, image, infrastructure and society. Through the concept of the mega-event legacy utopia, I also provide some insight toward the operationalization of the four urban traits for a city's economic development, local place marketing, urban development, and public participation.

Keywords: heterotopia, legacy, mega-event, Olympic, place, planning theory, society, transformation, urban theory, utopia.

Gotham, K. F. (2015). Beyond bread and circuses: Mega-events as forces of creative destruction. In *Mega-Events and Globalization* (pp. 43-59). Routledge.

Abstract: In this chapter, I use the concept of creative destruction to theorize the ways in which the planning and staging of mega-events reflect geographically uneven and politically volatile trajectories of urban development. Scholars such as David Harvey, Neil Smith and Neil Brenner have emphasized how the creative and destructive forces of capital have an impact on the built environment at various scales. The concept draws our attention to the ways in which capital seeks to destabilize and undermine inherited institutions and social structures that impede capital accumulation in order to facilitate new forms of investment and profit making. Creating and parceling out spaces for mega-events and associated urban redevelopment is tantamount to devaluing spaces in order to infuse them with value-producing potential. New transportation networks, water and energy infrastructures, information and communication technologies, and brick-and mortar projects for entertainment and consumption represent institutional efforts to enhance commodity exchange, create and diversify flows of investment, and promote the circulation of people, culture, and capital. Mega-event preparation activities typically anticipate and actively plan for the revalorization of space through displacement, rezoning, and the conversion of unprofitable land-uses into spaces of profit making via consumption-based entertainment experiences.

Chalkley, B. & Essex, S. (1999). Urban development through hosting international events: a history of the Olympic Games. *Planning perspectives,* **14**(4),
369-394.

Abstract: In recent years, there has been increased interest in the idea of promoting urban development and change through the hosting of major events.
This approach offers host cities the possibility of 'fast track' urban regeneration,
a stimulus to economic growth, improved transport and cultural facilities, and
enhanced global recognition and prestige. Many authors attribute the increased
importance of event-led development to wider transformations in the global
economy, such as post-Fordism and globalization. However, event-led development has a long history and can be recognized, for example, in the World Fairs
of the nineteenth century. The Olympic Games, the world's most prestigious
sporting event, has been held for over one hundred years with significant consequences for the host cities. This paper reviews the effects of the Olympics on the
urban environment of the various cities, which have acted as hosts in the modern
Olympic period (1896–1996). The material outlines the varied motivations for
staging the Games and examines their outcomes in terms of urban development.

4.4.6 Resources

Many managers would say this is the single most important area of concern,
as maintaining the resources necessary to produce events is absolutely critical.
For some events the key source of money is the customer, through ticket sales.
For others it is sponsors or grant-givers, and often it is a mix (Elbe, Axelsson
& Hallen, 2007). Festivals and events can fail if the necessary resources are not
provided by the event organizers (Getz, 2002). Resources required by the event
organizer include those shown in Figure 4.7.

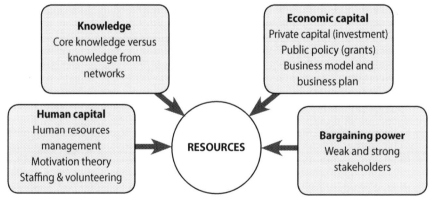

Figure 4.7: Resources

Human capital includes the necessary people with the necessary skill to organize and execute the event – people, including staff and volunteers, who are motivated to make the event successful. Staffing and volunteering will be discussed

in detail a little later. Internal staff will have **knowledge** but if there is a lack of knowledge in one specific area the necessary knowledge can be acquired from the network. Without the necessary funding events cannot be successful and the **economic capital** can be obtained from private investments or public grants. Not all events are profit driven (charity events) and with good business planning these events can be sustainable. **Bargain** with strong stakeholders to assist with the necessary resources to be successful.

Research note

Elbe, J., Axelsson, B., & Hallen, L. (2007). Mobilizing marginal resources for public events. *Event Management*, **10** (4), 175-183.

Abstract: Marginal resources are important for organizers of public events. In the present context, marginal resources are defined as resources that providers can offer to events in periods when these resources cannot be put to productive use in their regular operations. Such marginal resources are often mobilized through networks of social relationships when the resource providers regard a connection to the public event as being valuable. The mobilization of marginal resources is analyzed using a network approach and by analyzing the motives of the participating resource providers. Cases involving two public events are presented in order to illustrate the mobilization and the development of patterns and routines over time. The cases indicate that resources are mainly mobilized through networking. Building and using the legitimacy of the event are important factors in this process. The actors providing resources are motivated by a mix of interests, but most of them have an idealistic interest in the event. The mobilized resources are combined in ways that create economy of scope and scale for the organizer. Over time, a recurring event benefits from experience and learned behavior among the actors involved. It seems to be easier to mobilize resources in a community where the actors, and clusters of actors, are well connected with each other.

Keywords: Events, mobilization, resources, network, legitimacy

Getz, D. (2002). Why festivals fail. *Event management*, 7(4), 209-219.

Abstract: Exploratory research was conducted with festival management professionals to determine the incidence and causes of festival failure. Although the small sample does not permit generalization, results clearly reveal that festival crises and failures are common, and a number of likely sources of failure are identified: the weather; lack of corporate sponsorship; overreliance on one source of money; inadequate marketing or promotion; and lack of advance or strategic planning. A number of theoretical frameworks are examined that can help explain festival failure and shape further research, including resource dependency, Porter's framework for assessing competitive advantages, population ecology, and the product life cycle.

Keywords: Festival failure, management, resource dependency

4.4.7 Staffing and volunteers

Kim and Cuskelly (2017) indicate that events rely heavily on their volunteers and their commitment towards the event for the preparation and successful staging of the event. The appropriate recruitment strategies must be used to identify volunteers and factors influencing volunteer satisfaction should be identified to ensure volunteer retention (Pauline, 2011). Management practices and intrinsic motivation are important for volunteer engagement (Allen & Bartle, 2014). Volunteers are also strongly motivated by communication between them and the organizers, social contact and friendship, pride in culture and the country (Pauline, 2011). Other factors that motivate volunteers are external traditions, commitments, purposive and solidary (Farrell et al., 1998). Cuskelly et al. (2004) found in their research that volunteers can sometimes not be dependable when completing work assignments and that can influence the financial and operational success of major sport events. Event organizers should therefore monitor volunteers through their more permanent staff.

Research note

Pauline, G. (2011). Volunteer satisfaction and intent to remain: An analysis of contributing factors among professional golf event volunteers. *International Journal of Event Management Research*, **16**(1), 10-32.

Abstract: Sport events are increasingly reliant on episodic volunteers for the successful delivery of an event. As there continues to exist a surge in the organization of sporting events coupled with the demand for volunteers, event organizers must concern themselves with utilizing the appropriate recruitment and retention strategies. In an effort to do this, one must understand the points of satisfaction for volunteers as well as factors influencing their future intentions to volunteer. While there exists a plethora of research to understand the motivation of volunteers, exploring the antecedents of volunteer satisfaction as well as intent to remain has been limited. This study investigates the factors influencing volunteer satisfaction as well as intentions to remain as a volunteer for future sporting events from an elite men's golf event on the Professional Golf Association (PGA) circuit. Results indicated that overall volunteers were satisfied with their experience and willing to return yet were concerned with the level of communication between the organization and volunteers. The present study also found that longevity of service influenced volunteer satisfaction. A MANOVA revealed significant differences between first time and returning volunteers in their intent to continue volunteering for both sport events and community causes. The findings have implications to not only expand the theoretical understanding of sport volunteerism, but acknowledge the factors that sport event organizers need to concern themselves with relative to recruitment, management, and retention of volunteers for successful operations of events.

Keywords: Volunteer satisfaction, sport events, intent to remain

Allen, J. B. & Bartle, M. (2014). Sport event volunteers' engagement: management matters. *Managing Leisure*, **19**(1), 36-50.

Abstract: Volunteers are vital to the success of many major sporting events (Doherty, 2009). Understanding the factors that influence sport event volunteerism will assist in event volunteer management. This study used self-determination theory (Ryan & Deci, 2000) to examine the relationships among individuals' motivation for volunteering, perceptions of volunteer work climate and engagement. The participants were 44 marshals and scorers volunteering at the British Women's Golf Open, Carnoustie, Scotland 2011. They completed a questionnaire assessing their motivation for volunteering, perceptions of volunteer work climate, and psychological engagement whilst volunteering. Hierarchical regression analysis was used to examine the relationships among motivation, climate, and engagement. Volunteers' intrinsic motivation and perceptions of an autonomy-supportive work climate significantly predicted engagement. In conclusion, volunteers' engagement was related to their initial motivation, however, management practices were also important.

Keywords: volunteer motivation, engagement, autonomy support

Kim, E., & Cuskelly, G. (2017). A systematic quantitative review of volunteer management in events. *Event Management*, **21**(1), 83-100.

Abstract: Most event organizations rely on the commitment of volunteers to prepare for and stage events. An attempt to understand factors that affect volunteers' engagement and retention has received much attention from a substantial number of published studies. This article provides a systematic quantitative review of 71 original, peer-reviewed research articles published in English language academic journals on volunteer management in events. The review examines the nature of the research, methods, key concepts and theories, and types of research questions posed in studies associated with volunteer management in events. Published studies on event volunteer management are geographically concentrated in several countries but published in 35 different journals across a range of fields. Volunteer management in events has been the focus of rapidly increasing research attention in recent years with almost two thirds of the articles included in the review published in the 6 years leading to 2014. The majority of published research has not clearly articulated a theoretical framework and most studies have used survey methods to collect data from volunteers at mega-sport events. It was concluded that to advance knowledge of event volunteer management there is a need for increased collaboration internationally between researchers. Moreover, it is essential to engage with relevant theory in order to better understand and predict the effectiveness of volunteer management strategies in recruiting, retaining, and building a sense of community among volunteers in events.

Keywords: Volunteer management, Human resource management (HRM), Volunteers, events, review

4.5 The relevance of innovation diffusion theory

An innovation may be defined as something completely new, such as a product or method. But it is also a process of change management and can be deliberately fostered within an organization as part of its learning and problem-solving functions. Innovations tend to spread, sometimes very quickly, with stakeholders embedded in dense networks having an advantage in learning about and adopting new technologies or ideas (Larson, 2009; Mackellar, 2006). This applies within events and tourism, and might consist of new ways of employing social media for marketing and co-creation of experiences, or the use of festivals and events as instruments of innovation in community development.

The diffusion of innovation theory is attributed to Everett Rogers (2003) from a book named *Diffusion of Innovations*. He looked at how social systems affect diffusion, and suggested that the spread of a new idea was influenced by the idea/change/technology itself (just how appealing is it?), communication channels (the network), time, and the social system itself. Rogers also popularized the categorization of "innovators, early adopters, early majority, late majority, and laggards" for describing how certain people or groups learned about and used an innovation. Diffusion thus occurs over time, through geographic and social space, and is directly connected to social networks and stakeholder linkages.

Research notes

Larson, M. (2009). Festival innovation: Complex and dynamic network interaction. *Scandinavian Journal of Hospitality and Tourism, 9*(2-3), 288-307.

Abstract: This article argues that festival innovation is a highly cooperative endeavor among many actors in an inter-organizational network. The aim is to understand how collaborative festival innovation is performed and who takes part in the process. Material from case studies of three Swedish festivals showed that innovation takes place in complex networks involving many actors having various interests. Innovation networks are often highly dynamic and changing: innovation often takes place in new partnerships. The innovation work is hard to plan: it is to a large degree an emergent process and sometimes innovation originates from improvisation. Some innovation can, however, become institutionalized and embedded in the routines of the partnership interaction. Festival organizers need to reflect on their network and relate strategically to how their partners can contribute to successful festival innovation.

Keywords: Festival, innovation, network, complex and dynamic networks, emergent process

Mackellar, J. (2006). An integrated view of innovation emerging from a regional festival. *International Journal of Event Management Research*, **2** (1), 37-48.

Abstract: Scholars of economics, industrial systems and organizations have extensively examined the application of innovation theory in numerous economic environments and yet this adaptation has not been common in sociology. This paper reviews innovation theory in the context of a regional festival in NSW, Australia, where research has demonstrated the links between interactive network relationships and innovation. The research demonstrates an abundance of innovative activity that can occur at a regional event both from an economic and social perspective. It is suggested that a holistic typology may be useful for researchers and regional planners to more closely examine the characteristics of innovation occurring in a regional community.

Keywords: Innovation, network, festival

Discussion questions

1 Provide examples of issues or problems involving stakeholders, and suggested solutions, to demonstrate your understanding of how to apply stakeholder theory to the following management functions:
   ☐ Organizing and planning
   ☐ Sustainability
   ☐ Marketing and branding
   ☐ Experiences of all stakeholders
   ☐ Impacts and evaluation
   ☐ Resources

Assessment activities

Try to evaluate economic, social, cultural, ecological/ environmental and built environment impacts of a planned event as if you were the organizer. After that evaluate the event's efficiency from the perspectives of different stakeholders.

Recommended additional reading and sources

Getz, D. (2018). Event Evaluation: *Theory and Methods for Event Management and Tourism*. Oxford: Goodfellow Publishers.

Getz, D. (2018). *Event Impact Assessment: Theory and Methods for Event Management and Tourism*. Oxford: Goodfellow Publishers.

Hede, A,M. (2007). Managing special events in the new era of the triple bottom line. *Event Management*, **11** (1-2), 13-22.

References

Allen, J. B. & Bartle, M. (2014). Sport event volunteers' engagement: management matters. *Managing Leisure*, **19**(1), 36-50.

Azzali, S. (2017). Mega-events and urban planning: Doha as a case study. *Urban Design International*, **22**(1), 3-12.

Beard, C. & Russ, W. (2017). Event evaluation and design: Human experience mapping. *Event Management*, **21**, 365–374.

Buch, T., Milne, S. & Dickson, G. (2011). Multiple stakeholder perspectives on cultural events: Auckland's Pasifika Festival. *Journal of Hospitality Marketing & Management*, **20**(3-4), 311-328.

Chalkley, B. & Essex, S. (1999). Urban development through hosting international events: a history of the Olympic Games. *Planning perspectives*, **14**(4), 369-394.

Coetser, J. (2002). *The South African War: Occasion and event in Afrikaans theatre*. Retrieved from http://www.childlit.org.za/KonfBoerCoetser.html

Collins, A., Jones, C. & Munday, M. (2009). Assessing the environmental impacts of mega sporting events: Two options? *Tourism Management*, **30**(6), 828-837.

Curtis, J., Hynes, S., O'Reilly, P. & Breen, B. (2017). Recreational angling tournaments: Participants' expenditures. *Journal of Sport & Tourism*, **21** (3), 201–221.

Cuskelly, G., Auld, C., Harrington, M. & Coleman, D. (2004). Predicting the behavioral dependability of sport event volunteers. *Event Management*, **9**(1-2), 73-89.

Elbe, J., Axelsson, B. & Hallen, L. (2007). Mobilizing marginal resources for public events. *Event Management*, **10** (4), 175-183.

Farrell, J. M., Johnston, M. E. & Twynam, G. D. (1998). Volunteer motivation, satisfaction, and management at an elite sporting competition. *Journal of Sport Management*, **12**(4), 288-300.

Fenich, G. G. (2013). *Meetings, Expositions, Events & Conventions: Pearson New International Edition: An Introduction to the Industry*. Pearson Higher Ed.

Getz, D. (2002). Why festivals fail. *Event management*, **7**(4), 209-219.

Getz, D. (2013). *Event tourism: concepts, international case studies, and research*. Cognizant Communication Corporation.

Getz, D. (2018). *Event Evaluation: Theory and Methods for Event Management and Tourism*. Oxford: Goodfellow Publishers.

Getz, D. (2018). *Event Impact Assessment: Theory and Methods for Event Management and Tourism*. Oxford: Goodfellow Publishers.

Getz, D., & Andersson, T. D. (2008). Sustainable festivals: On becoming an institution. *Event Management*, **12**(1), 1-17.

Getz, D., & Andersson, T. (2010). The event-tourist career trajectory: A study of high-involvement amateur distance runners. *Scandinavian Journal of Tourism and Hospitality*, **19** (4), 468-491.

Getz, D., & McConnell, A. (2014). Comparing runners and mountain bikers on involvement and event-travel careers. *Journal of Convention and Event Tourism,* **15** (1), 69-100.

Getz, D., & McConnell, A. (2011). Serious sport tourism and event travel careers. *Journal of Sport Management,* **25** (4), 326-338.

Getz, D. and Page, S. (2016) *Event Studies, Theory, Research and Policy for Planned Events,* 3rd ed. London: Routledge

Gotham, K. F. (2015). Beyond bread and circuses: Mega-events as forces of creative destruction. In *Mega-Events and Globalization* (pp. 43-59). Routledge.

Grimble, R. & Wellard, K. (1997). Stakeholder methodologies in natural resource management: a review of principles, contexts, experiences and opportunities. *Agricultural Systems,* **55**(2), 173-193.

Guizzardi, A., Mariani, M. & Prayag, G. (2017). Environmental impacts and certification: evidence from the Milan World Expo 2015. *International Journal of Contemporary Hospitality Management,* **29**(3), 1052-1071.

Hall, C. M. & Hodges, J. (1996). The party's great, but what about the hangover?: The housing and social impacts of mega-events with special reference to the 2000 Sydney Olympics. *Festival Management and Event Tourism,* **4**(1-1), 13-20.

Hard, R. (2018). What do destination management companies (DMCs) do? Retrieved from www.thebalancesmb.com/what-do-destination-management -companies-dmcs-do-1223653

Hauptfleisch, T. 2006. Identity: Festivals in South Africa and the search for cultural identity. *New Theatre Quarterly,* **22**, 181–198.

IBM Center for the Business of Government. (2018). *Inter-organizational Networks: A review of the literature to inform practice.* Washington DC: Washington

Jackson, L. A. (2008). Residents' perceptions of the impacts of special event tourism. *Journal of Place Management and Development,* **1**(3), 240-255.

Karlsen, S., & Stenbacka Nordström, C. (2009). Festivals in the Barents Region: Exploring Festival-stakeholder Cooperation. *Scandinavian Journal of Hospitality and Tourism,* **9**(2-3), 130-145.

Kassens-Noor, E. (2016). From ephemeral planning to permanent urbanism: An urban planning theory of mega-events. *Urban Planning,* **1**(1), 41-54.

Kim, E., & Cuskelly, G. (2017). A systematic quantitative review of volunteer management in events. *Event Management,* **21**(1), 83-100.

Larson, M. (1997). *Evenemangsmarknadsföring—organisering, styrning och samverkan vid marknadsföringen av VM i friidrott 1995.* Östersund: Tryckeribolaget Östersund AB.

Larson M. (2000). Interaction in the political market square: Organising marketing of events. In R. A. Lundin & F. Hartman (Eds.), *Projects as Business Constituents and Guiding Motives.* pp. 167–180. Massachusetts: Kluwer Academic Publishers.

Larson, M. (2009). Festival innovation: Complex and dynamic network interaction. *Scandinavian Journal of Hospitality and Tourism,* **9**(2-3), 288-307.

Larson, M. & Wikström, E. (2001). Organizing events: Managing conflict and consensus in a political market square. *Event Management*, **7**(1), 51-65.

Leopkey, B. & Parent, M. M. (2009). Risk management issues in large-scale sporting events: A stakeholder perspective. *European Sport Management Quarterly*, **9**(2), 187-208.

Liu, D. (2016). Social impact of major sports events perceived by host community. *International Journal of Sports Marketing and Sponsorship*, **17**(1), 78-91.

Mackellar, J. (2006). An integrated view of innovation emerging from a regional festival. *International Journal of Event Management Research*, **2** (1), 37-48.

Mossberg, L., & Getz, D. (2006). Stakeholder influences on the ownership and management of festival brands. *Scandinavian Journal of Hospitality and Tourism*, **6**(4), 308-326.

Pauline, G. (2011). Volunteer satisfaction and intent to remain: An analysis of contributing factors among professional golf event volunteers. *International Journal of Event Management Research*, **16**(1) 10-32.

Pfeffer J. & Salancik G. (1978). *The External Control of Organizations: A resource dependence pwerspective*. Harper Row

Prebensen, N. (2010). Value creation through stakeholder participation: a case study of an event In The High North. *Event Management*, **14** (1), 37-52.

Presbury, R., & Edwards, D. C. (2005). Incorporating sustainability in meetings and event management education. *International Journal of Event Management Research*, **1**(1), 30-45.

Robertson, M. & Rogers, P. (2009). Festivals, cooperative stakeholders and the role of the media: A case analysis of newspaper media. *Scandinavian Journal of Hospitality and Tourism*, **9**(2-3), 206-224.

Rogers, E. M. (2003). *Diffusion of Innovations*, 5th edition, Free Press.

Savage, G., Nix, T., Whitehead, C. & Blair, J. (1991). Strategies for assessing and managing organizational stakeholders. *Academy of Management Executive*, **5** (2), 61-75.

Schein, E. (1992). *Organizational Culture and Leadership: A Dynamic View*. San Francisco, CA: Jossey-Bass.

Schlenker, K., Edwards, D. C. & Sheridan, L. (2005). A flexible framework for evaluating the socio-cultural impacts of a small festival. *International Journal of Event Management Research*, **1**(1), 66-77.

Scott, W. R. (2004). Institutional theory, in G. Ritzer, ed. *Encyclopedia of Social Theory*, P408-14 Thousand Oaks, CA: Sage.

Scudder, S.F. (1980). Communication Theory as a Universal Law.

Smelser, N. J., & Baltes, P. B. (Eds.). (2001). *International Encyclopedia of the Social & Behavioral Sciences* (Vol. 11). Amsterdam: Elsevier.

Solomon , M. R. & Buchanan, B. (1991), A role theoretic approach to product symbolism-mapping a consumption constellation, *Journal of Business Research*, **22**, 95-109.

Spiropoulos, S., Gargalianos, D. & Sotiriadou, K. (2005). The 20th Greek festival of Sydney: a stakeholder analysis. *Event Management*, **9**(4), 169-183.

Tkaczynski, A. (2013). A stakeholder approach to attendee segmentation: A case study of an Australian Christian music festival. *Event Management*, **17** (3), 283-298.

Van Niekerk, M., & Coetzee, W. J. L. (2011). Utilizing the VICE model for the sustainable development of the Innibos Arts Festival. *Journal of Hospitality Marketing & Management*, **20** (3-4), 347-365.

Wang, Y., & Pizam, A. (Eds.). (2011). *Tourism Destination Marketing and Management: Collaborative Stratagies*. CABI.

5 Stakeholder Considerations for Different Types of Event

Learning objectives

At the end of the chapter readers should understand how stakeholder theory applies to the management of various types of planned event, namely:

☐ Sports

☐ Festivals

☐ Business events

☐ Entertainment

☐ Mega events

☐ Hallmark events

☐ Iconic events

5.1 Introduction

Every event manager will face some different stakeholder issues and come up with a wide variety of individualistic strategies, but there are going to be commonalities among the major types of event, and these are considered in this chapter.

Planned events are most frequently classified by reference to their *form*, since it is usually obvious that sport events are visibly different from festivals, and meetings are quite different in structure and program from exhibitions. But an additional consideration, already noted in this book, is the *function* of events. This chapter therefore includes a discussion of mega events (the largest), hallmark events (permanent institutions, co-branded with cities and destinations) and iconic events (holding symbolic importance to special-interest groups).

What are the stakeholder-related variables that are important when looking at forms and functions? These are the main ones:

♦ **Mandate or purpose**: Obviously there will be major differences between stakeholders if the event is service- versus profit-oriented, and if the event can determine its own strategies as opposed to being subsumed under another agency or corporation and its strategy.

♦ **Who is important?** e.g., for sport events, teams, clubs and athletes are critical stakeholders, as are sport governing bodies; for festivals, the performers or artists are essential, as are volunteers.

♦ **Distribution of power**: Major sport events are 'owned' by international bodies, and they have bargaining power; festivals often depend upon local authorities and grants from government agencies; private events have to sell tickets to customers, so power relationships change with the event and its setting.

♦ **Scale**: mega events are large, expensive, complex and generate many outcomes – some will be perceived to be good, and others not; the distribution of costs and benefits is a critical issue related to stakeholders. Many events are so small that they are not in themselves of interest to many possible stakeholder groups. Scale also affects media coverage and political oversight.

♦ **Location**: Where events are held is an important variable, as those living and doing business nearby are likely to be most affected; indoor venues are generally less likely to annoy neighbors or cause environmental damage than events held in parks (although construction and land-use changes must be evaluated).

♦ **Audience**: Does the event generate large demand from participants or spectators, or is it for invited guests only? Do they travel by car or public transit? Is the event dependent upon ticket sales or participant fees? These variables help determine stakeholder salience.

♦ **Frequency**: Regularly held sport events and festivals give rise to predictable impacts, while one-time events carry additional risks and deserve greater scrutiny by more stakeholders. Periodic events can sort out stakeholder issues over time, leading to smoother operations.

5.2 Key terms defined

Mega-events

"Mega-events are ambulatory occasions of a fixed duration that attract a large number of visitors, have a large mediated reach, come with large costs and have large impacts on the built environment and the population" Müller (2015:638). Getz (2013) argued that while 'mega' usually applies to the biggest events, such as the Olympics,

World's Fairs or World Cup, it is actually a relative concept, as even small events can stretch the capacity of a venue or place heavy burdens on a community, therefore being 'mega' in particular contexts.

Hallmark events

"Hallmark tourist events are major fairs, expositions, cultural and sporting events of international status which are held on either a regular or a one-off basis. A primary function of the hallmark event is to provide the host community with an opportunity to secure high prominence in the tourism market place. However, international or regional prominence may be gained with significant social and environmental costs" Hall (1989:263). Getz et al. (2012) provided a planning model for hallmark events, and noted (p. 50) *"Almost all examples given of hallmark events are of permanent, periodic events that are sports and cultural celebrations and often combined."* Hallmark events tend to be viewed as institutions meeting multiple goals, co-branded with their host city or destination, and deserving of rescue if they are threatened.

Iconic events

"Hallmark events by their nature are iconic. The core meaning of iconic is that of a symbol, or something possessing symbolic value ... Levy (2007), referring to news rather than planned events, described iconic events as those which gain mythic status within a culture, related to their newsworthiness followed by extensive interpretation and exploitation in political arenas. Applied to hallmark events, the implication is that they have to continuously attract media attention and enter into the realm of popular, if not political discourse. However, a more pertinent concept is that of 'cultural icon'." As quoted by Getz et al. (2012:51).

5.3   Case study: The Volga Boat Show, Russia

Maksim V. Godovykh – Rosen College of Hospitality Management – USA

The Volga Boat Show is one of the major yachting trade fairs in Russia. It takes place in Samara region at the ultramodern yacht port Druzba, and the program includes both in water and land expositions, test-drives, presentations, trainings, regatta and water sport competitions, concerts, art gallery, and even an air show. The show is organized by Premium Event LLC and annually gathers more than 5,000 visitors from different parts of Russia and other countries. Since the Volga Boat Show is a multi-faced event, its organizing process involves various stakeholders from government and municipal authorities, sport federations and professional associations, boat manufacturers and distributors, sponsors and partners, mass media and social network groups. Besides that, attendees also have completely different motives for visiting the event and can be divided into three main categories: potential buyers; knowledge seekers, or people aimed at attending trainings, seminars, and presentations; and family groups mostly interested in having a good time with their children.

Photo 5.1: The Volga Boat Show. Picture credit: Maksim V. Godovykh

The most important external stakeholder for Russian major events is the **Government**. Usually it is difficult to involve it in the organizing process, but it really helps to promote events and to attract other important groups of stakeholders: exponents, partners, visitors. Besides, organizing water events demands a vast number of permits and approvals from transportation police, water safety department, municipal authorities, emergency aid department, rescue services and other institutions. Hence, having officials as part of the organizing team helps to coordinate all the tasks in the fastest and most efficient way. The most effective way to convince the Government to support an event is to present economic benefits for the region, including attracting external and foreign visitors, signing agreements, and attracting investments. It might be also a good idea to include representatives of executive and legislative bodies in the organizing committee. The Volga Boat Show annually conducts three official sessions with authorities, responsible for safety and authorizing documentation. The first meeting usually takes place three months prior to the event, the second session – one month beforehand, and the third one is held during the last week of preparatory phase. The main objectives of these gatherings are to assign areas of responsibility and to control readiness. Organization team also holds press conferences with ministers, deputies, local authorities, and invites them to the formal opening of the Volga Boat Show.

The next important stakeholder category is **exhibitors**. The best way to start working with them is to contact them directly. The Volga Boat Show sales people usually start their activity ten months before the event, by sending emails and phoning international manufacturers of yachts, boats, engines, spare parts, equipment, as well as international federations and associations. After that the Volga Boat Show managers personally meet with potential participants during the biggest international events in Monaco, Cannes, Amsterdam, and Dusseldorf. Then the work with national manufacturers and distributors begins from receiving references from their headquarters and foreign partners. The last wave of selling activity is related to inviting associated industries like car dealers, banks, real estate developers etc. Potential participants usually ask for event data on the number of attendees, signed contracts, logistics, safety, and event promotion in order to calculate their ROI. However, it is possible to offer discounts or free options in order to attract industry leaders during the first years of organizing a new event from scratch. The Volga Boat Show initially provided discounted participation plans for main players like famous luxury yacht manufacturers, sport car brands, helicopter and aircraft companies, which always attract additional attendees, and which are usually followed by zealous participants.

One more important group of stakeholders is **partners and sponsors**. The majority of boat show partners in Russia comes from the financial sector, car manufacturing, insurance, and mobile services. On the one hand, they provide a considerable part of funding. On the other hand, sponsors usually try to remake the program, include their own activities, place-oversized banners, and forbid physical presence of their competitors. The best advice for organizers is not to follow partners' caprices. Each event has a plan of preparation activities, exhibition diagrams, meetings schedule and other pre-agreed documents, and it is not a good idea to change these plans under the influence of external stakeholders, especially during the last phases of preparation process. In the meantime, usually it can be beneficial to incorporate general partners in the promotion campaign for the next year and design new events that meet the sponsor's objectives and requirements.

Photo 5.2: The Volga Boat Show. Picture credit: Maksim V. Godovykh

The hallmark of the Volga Boat Show is the strong promotion campaign based on mutually beneficial relations with **mass media stakeholders**. Hundreds of information sources are interested in supporting major events and promoting their services to affluent audience of potential yacht buyers and boat show visitors. The majority of major yacht magazines, websites, and social media groups supported the Volga Boat Show for free as organizers provided content, pictures, videos, and narratives. Regional TV channels, radios, newspapers, billboards, and news media promoted the Volga Boat Show at no charge as a remarkable event for the area. International and national associations and federations also support the show by spreading information among its members and partners. Cross promotion turned out to be the most efficient way of promoting the event. The Volga Boat Show as a large venue with dozens of floors and meetings managed to provide space for numerous partners' activities including seminars, conferences, presentations, shows, lotteries and many others. In return, partners also promoted the show and bought their attendees to the major floor. As a result, the Volga Boat Show received unprecedented media coverage by letting media partners promote themselves during the event.

Photo 5.3: The Volga Boat Show. Picture credit: Maksim V. Godovykh

Every significant event should be supported by the **local community** in order to be successful. The Volga Boat Show organizers take every effort in order to make their event important, memorable, and beneficial for local people. First of all, the business program is diversified with concerts, sport competitions, art galleries, educational events, air shows and many other activities that make them real high days for the whole city. Second, the Volga Boat Show hosts a children's program during the last day of the event. All kids enter for free and can familiarize themselves with different types of yachts and boats, basics of boating, sailors' knots rope work, animated cartoon production, drawing, dancing, playing music instruments etc. The Volga Boat Show sailing regatta is for children from 5 to 16 years, and offers an opportunity to win a new small sailing boat. Besides that, all transportation, housing, and food options, offered by local businesses are supported by the organizing committee and promoted on the Volga Boat Show website, in printing materials, and social networks.

Understanding the motives of all stakeholders and setting relations on a mutually beneficial basis allowed the Volga Boat Show to become a major yachting event in Russia from the first year of its existence. The Government support facilitated the process of receiving permits, highest level of safety, and perfect promotion. Good relations with manufacturers, associations, industry leaders, and partners lead to larger number of exponents and eventful program of the show, and fulfilling needs of the cross promotion partners factor into huge media coverage. As a result, the Volga Boat Show received the Best Russian Business Event Award on the second year of its operation.

5.4 Stakeholder management for sport events

In this section we consider organized sport events, from the smallest youth sport festivals held in neighborhood parks, to the professional sports held in large-scale arenas and stadia. There are big differences between regularly-scheduled sport events and one-time events that have to be bid on competitively. Participation events are quite different from spectator-oriented or media events. Mega events are given their own section later. A number of stakeholders are particular to most sport events, namely athletes, sport clubs, teams, and governing/sanctioning bodies. Sport-specific venues take on a higher importance (i.e., the need for tennis, football ice hockey arenas, etc.), as do officials. Sport media are different than general media, especially because of the television networks devoted to sports.

Sport events are global in significance and often form the foundation of event-tourism strategies. This has given rise to sport development and/or sport tourism agencies being an essential part of tourism in most North American cities. Because there are innumerable sport events occurring locally and regionally (in numbers this is dominated by amateurs and youth), even small jurisdictions can build facilities and compete for business. Major and international sport events are usually bid on competitively.

Figure 5.1 identifies the major stakeholder groups being considered, with the event being in the center as the focal organization.

Of special importance in this discussion is the *Routledge Handbook of Sports Event Management* (Chappelet & Parent, 2015) which takes a stakeholder perspective throughout. Specific attention in that book is given to event organizers, sport organizations, the participants (i.e. athletes), support groups including parents and delegations, the host community including government and tourism, funders and sponsors, media including social media, and other stakeholders such as security and non-governmental organizations. Note that not all of these stakeholder groups are defined by function, and suppliers will fall under host community or the supporter role.

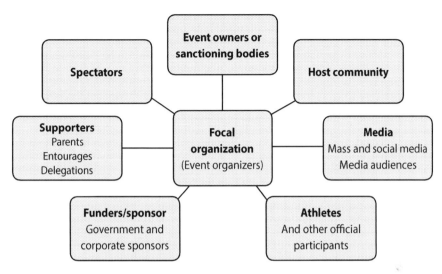

Figure 5.1: Major stakeholder groups. Source: Adapted from Chappelet & Parent (2015).

We will discuss all of them in detail later in the chapter. When stakeholders all work together it is possible that events can cause certain behavior changes in the local community. For instance, sport events can be used to increase the participation rate in sports after the sport event has left town (Misener et al., 2015).

Research note

Misener, L., Taks, M., Chalip, L. & Green, B. C. (2015). The elusive 'trickle-down effect' of sport events: Assumptions and missed opportunities. *Managing Sport and Leisure*, **20**(2), 135-156.

Abstract: The claimed benefits of sport events on sport participation rely on an asserted 'trickle-down effect'. There is a lack of empirical evidence that events can trigger increased physical activity and sport participation, and research has focused on large-scale events. This paper compares two previously hosted medium-sized sport events, and examines the degree to which local (sport) organizations and local organizing committees (LOC) endeavoured to leverage each sport event for sport participation purposes. Document analysis and semi-structured interviews revealed overarching assumptions that the events in and of themselves were sufficient to engender participation outcomes. Strategies for leveraging were absent, and only a few tactics were identified. Leverage could come from augmented exposure via amplified media, celebrations, further demonstrations of the sport, and teaching about the sport. A key constraint is identifying who should be responsible for implementing and executing the leveraging strategy and tactics. The findings inform various stakeholders – event organizers, sport organizations, and local communities, to find ways to use events as a lever for sport participation by making it a part of their overall marketing efforts.

Keywords: sport event, leverage, legacy, strategy, sport participation

5.4.1 Bidding on events

It is essential to go beyond the identification of stakeholder groups and their main roles to examine the nature of relationships and how they can be or should be managed. That can be a complex process requiring stakeholder mapping by those who know the way things actually work and can draw upon experience to critically evaluate mistakes, issues and opportunities for improvement. Within the sports realm one of the more complex processes involving many stakeholders is that of bidding on events.

A key stakeholder management issue is the event bidding process which occurs in a special marketplace consisting of owners, bidders/buyers, and inter-mediaries. Getz (2004) modeled this marketplace, as illustrated in Figure 5.2, including bid success factors. Emery (2002) has examined bidding in a stake-holder context, adding 'intermediaries and agencies' and stressing 'conflict issues' in the process.

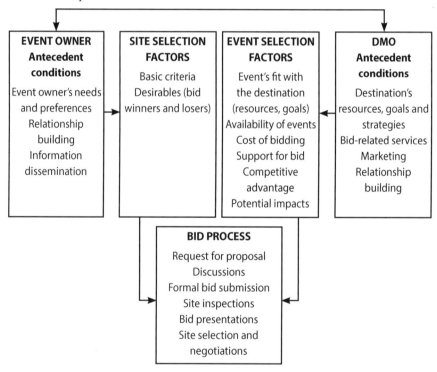

Figure 5.2: Event bidding process. Source: Adapted from Getz (2004).

Hautbois, Parent & Seguin (2012) offer some criteria that can be implemented for a successful bid but also consider the stakeholder network as a key factor. They also look at the salience of different stakeholder relationships and deter-mine the bid success factor. All stakeholders should work together for the bid to be successful. Lockstone-Binney et al. (2014) investigated in their study how ambassador programs worldwide can influence, high-profile individuals to award the bids to the bidding organization. Owners of events, or the sanctioning bodies, have a great deal of power when many bidders get involved, but their power diminishes when the event has been awarded and local/national consortia have to produce it on time (and hopefully within budget). If event organizers cannot produce it on time, or run out of money, the owners have a major problem.

On the bidders' side, who actually makes the bid is often less important than who has the power to sanction or reject a bid, and while this powerful actor is often local government (who are owners of venues, regulators of land use and necessary funders) it might also be national governments (who must be part of Olympic bids), or the venues needed for competitions. When infrastructure is required, such as new sport venues or transportation improvements, additional funds and multiple approvals are required government plays an important role.

Community support or opposition are often determining factors, with mega-events and their costs attracting the most attention and generating the most controversy. 'Power to the people' rings true in those cases where citizens are organized in their opposition, and the media can also have a substantial effect on decision-makers by either giving tacit or explicit support, or taking the role of opponent. In their book *Event Bidding*, McGillivray and Turner (2018) critically discuss the reasons for bidding, mega-event impacts, and growing resistance to the pro-development powers that have sustained the trend to bigger and costlier events.

Research note

Emery, P. R. (2002). Bidding to host a major sports event: The local organising committee perspective. *International Journal of Public Sector Management*, 15(4), 316-335.

Abstract: Major sports events have the potential to offer significant benefits to any city, but at the same time are likely to entail immense resource utilisation and enormous risk. Focussed at the organising committee level, and drawing upon general management and project management literature, aims to collect empirical data to identify current management practice used in the bidding process, and determine key factors in successful bidding. A self-administered postal questionnaire was sent to 220 randomly selected major sports event organisers from ten different countries. Targeted at the chief executive officer level or equivalent, the questionnaire provided general contextual detail and focussed on present sports event management practices and processes. To gain more in-depth understanding of successful applications, three semi-structured interviews were administered in England. The findings reveal that the primary motivations behind local authority involvement are heightening area profile and sport promotion. Successful public sector applications were found to use bounded rational decision-making, driven largely by political reasoning rather than detailed objective analysis. Specifically identifies and discusses five key factors behind successful national and international governing body approval.

Keywords: Sport, tendering, marketing

Lockstone-Binney, L., Whitelaw, P., Robertson, M., Junek, O. & Michael, I. (2014). The motives of ambassadors in bidding for international association meetings and events. *Event Management*, **18**(1), 65-74.

Abstract: As destinations contest the rights to host international association-based meetings and events, competitive points of difference in the bidding process can mean the success or loss of a bid. One of these points of difference has been the growth of ambassador programs worldwide. These programs consist of influential, high-profile individuals, representing their particular industry body or association. Ambassadors work together with destination marketing organizations (DMOs) and meetings/conference professionals in putting forward bids to their association for future events. To understand the motivations of ambassadors in bidding for international meetings and events, an exploratory study employing an online survey was conducted with ambassadors from three programs, one based in Australia, one based in Southeast Asia, and one in the Middle East. The results provide a demographic profile of ambassadors and highlight their motives for actively bidding for international meetings and events. The study adds to knowledge on a topic for which limited research has been undertaken—that of the bidding process for business events—and expands understanding of how ambassador programs, together with DMOs, can contribute to a professional bidding process for globally roaming international association meetings and events.

Keywords: ambassador programs; bidding; business events; destination marketing organizations (DMOs)

Hautbois, C., Parent, M. M., & Séguin, B. (2012). How to win a bid for major sporting events? A stakeholder analysis of the 2018 Olympic Winter Games French bid. *Sport Management Review*, *15*(3), 263-275.

Abstract: While understanding the planning and hosting of major sporting events is a popular research area, less is known about the bid process despite the potential economic and political spinoffs. Some studies offer criteria for successful bids and even consider the stakeholder network as a key factor. Considering the importance of the stakeholder network, we delve deeper into this area. Using the power, legitimacy and urgency framework by Mitchell et al. (1997), we examine the 2018 Olympic Winter Games' French national bid competition (four candidacies) to analyze the stakeholder relationships, identify their salience and then determine stakeholder-based bid key success factors. Archival material and 28 interviews were analyzed. We notably found that to increase the probability of winning, no actor alone should have a definitive status, the sport stakeholder group should have at least the expectant status, and no strategic stakeholder should have the latent status. We also find that a three-level analysis of the stakeholder network allows for a greater understanding of the bid governance and process dynamics at play, which help to elucidate a successful bid. We contribute to the literature by (a) showing how stakeholder salience analysis can assist in understanding the bid network governance structure; (b) demonstrating that stakeholder salience depends on the level which is analyzed (local, between bids, and with the event owner), the stage (deciding to bid, national bid competition, national bid win/international competition), and the case/context; and (c) determining stakeholder-based key bid success factors such as who should and should not be more salient in the bid process.

Keywords: Major sporting events, stakeholder, Olympic Games, bid

5.4.2 Focal organization

Looking back at the major stakeholders as identified by Chappelet & Parent (2015) in Figure 5.1, the first stakeholder group we will discuss is the focal organization. This is the organization or collaborating group with strategic goals and responsible for the event production. Depending on the type of event the focal organization will be different. In the case of mega-events local government becomes the focal organization, as they are responsible for signing the host-city agreement with event owners and is also responsible for executing it.

In the study of Parent & Séguin (2007) the event owners cancelled the contract with the organizing committee due to a lack of financial commitment, power struggle between partners, politics and communication to name a few. The focal organization can either conform to certain pressures or resist them depending on the situation (Parent & Slack, 2007).

Research note

Parent, M., & Séguin, B. (2007). Factors that led to the drowning of a world championship organizing committee: A stakeholder approach. *European Sport Management Quarterly, 7*(2), 187-212.

Abstract: The purpose of this paper was to explore the organizational and stakeholder-related factors which led to the Fédération Internationale de Natation (FINA) cancelling its contract with the 2005 Montreal Aquatics World Championships Organizing Committee, thereby pulling the event from Montreal, Canada. The case study, based on stakeholder theory, was built through bid/organizing committee member and stakeholder interviews and archival material. A lack of formal financial commitments, power congruence between partners and the pervasive politics, communication, proper human resource management procedures, and proper due diligence emerged as the critical combination of factors which resulted in the unfortunate outcome. This study contributes significantly to the literature and to entities/stakeholders engaged in events (governments, sport federations, etc.) by (1) providing a new approach to studying failed organizing committees; and (2) highlighting issues that are critical to managing (and keeping) sporting events, thus avoiding failure. A model of organizing committee failure is also proposed.

Keywords: Stakeholders, stakeholder theory, event organizer, 2005 FINA World Championships

Parent, M. & Slack, T. (2007). Conformity and resistance: Preparing a Francophone sporting eEvent in North America. *Event Management*, **11**(3), 129-143.

Abstract: Organizing committees of large-scale sporting events face conflicting pressures from their environment when preparing to host the events, thereby leading them to conform to certain pressures and resist others. Writers on organizations, primarily institutional theorists, have mainly examined conformity, not resistance. This article seeks to examine the competing conforming and resistance pressures for an organizing committee. Findings from a case study relating to the Jeux de la Francophonie, or Games of La Francophonie, highlighted the presence of conflicting pressures between the North American context of the organizing committee and the European, Francophonie context of the event's international body, which impacted goal setting, funding/commercialization, athlete/artist caliber, sanctioning, and international government relationship and VIP treatment. The nature of the event, the stakeholders involved, and the event's setting or context were found to be interrelated sources of pressures on the organizing committee.

Keywords: case study, conformity, events, francophone, francophonie, institutional theory, pressure, resistance, stakeholders

5.4.3 The event owners/sanctioning bodies

Event owners have a responsibility towards the community where the event takes place and need to follow proper management practices (Walters & Tacon, 2010). Many event owners understand this corporate social responsibility (CSR) and have implemented various programs and projects to give back to the communities where they operate. Bradish & Cronin (2009) investigate some of these projects in their article on CSR within sport and gives examples how Sports Philanthropy Project, Right to Play and FIFA have given back to the communities.

Research note

Walters, G., & Tacon, R. (2010). Corporate social responsibility in sport: Stakeholder management in the UK football industry. *Journal of Management & Organization*, **16**(4), 566-586.

Abstract: Corporate social responsibility (CSR) has become increasingly significant for a wide range of organisations and for the managers that work within them. This is particularly true in the sport industry, where CSR is now an important area of focus for sport organisations, sport events and individual athletes. This article demonstrates how CSR can inform both theoretical debates and management practice within sport organisations. It does so by focusing on stakeholder theory, which overlaps considerably with CSR. In this article, stakeholder theory is used to examine three major CSR issues: stakeholder definition and salience, firm actions and responses, and stakeholder actions and responses. These three issues are considered in the context of the UK football industry. The article draws on 15 semi-structured qualitative interviews with senior representatives from a number of different organisations. These include the director of a large professional football club; a chief executive of a medium-sized professional football club in addition to the supporter-elected director; and the vice-chairman of a small professional football club. Additional interviews were undertaken with five representatives from national supporter organisations, two board members at two large supporter associations, two representatives from the Football League, one representative from the Independent Football Commission, and a prominent sports journalist. The analysis of the interview data illustrates ways in which CSR can be implemented by sport organisations through stakeholder management strategies. The article concludes that stakeholder theory has both conceptual and empirical value and can be used to illuminate key issues in sport management.

Keywords: corporate social responsibility, stakeholder theory, stakeholder salience, stakeholder management, sport organisations, football

5.4.4 Host community

Events have positive and negative impacts on the host community where they are being held and the perceived impacts of the events are likely to be modifiable with the passage of time (Kim & Petrick, 2005). We have discussed these impacts in detail in Chapter 4. Sport events have been used in urban development, the construction of major sport facilities (Friedman & Mason, 2004) and the possibility of forming community networks has been explored (Misener & Mason, 2006).

Involving residents has become extremely important specifically during mega-events and most mega-events are sport events. As previously mentioned, during mega-events government takes the role of the focal organization and Chi, Ouyang and Xu (2018) focus on how the local residents subjectively evaluate the event and how this influence their attitude towards it. The host community can also be consulted to understand if they would like to see a specific sport event to grow or not (Moital, Jackson & Le Couillard, 2013).

Research note

Chi, C. G. Q., Ouyang, Z., & Xu, X. (2018). Changing perceptions and reasoning process: Comparison of residents' pre-and post-event attitudes. *Annals of Tourism Research*, **70**, 39-53.

Abstract: Upon a systematic assessment of how residents' trust in government(s) and attachment to a marquee event influence their evaluations of the event's impacts and subsequent attitudes towards the hosting of the event, this study further explores the dynamic nature of residents' subjective evaluations and corresponding attitudes to the event. In line with the confirmation bias theory, findings clearly demonstrate that residents' trust in government(s), attachment to the event, perceptions of the event's impacts and ultimate support to the event have changed in a predictable manner over time. Moreover, findings indicate that individuals' direct experience with the event alters the associations between their cognitive/affective evaluations and attitudes towards it, with a shifted focus to the cognitive evaluations after the event.

Keywords: Temporal change, confirmation bias, tourism impacts, event attachment, political trust

Moital, I., Jackson, C. & Le Couillard, J. (2013). Using scenarios to investigate stakeholders' views on the future of a sporting event. *Event Management*, **17**, (4), 439-452.

Abstract: The aim of this research was to identify if the continuation of a sporting event was supported by its stakeholders and what their objectives were for its future. Using a methodology adapted from scenario planning, the research investigated if the stakeholders desired the event to grow, and if so, in which areas and to what level. The finding was that the stakeholders supported its growth. They viewed the sporting event as being a small-scale to medium-scale event and saw it growing to become a medium- to large-scale event. A key finding was that the stakeholders had conflicting views about its future features, and this was due to their varying backgrounds and objectives set for the event. The results of this research emphasize the need for both researchers and practitioners to be more fully aware of the similarities and differences in stakeholder objectives in a dynamic, rather than static, environment.

Keywords: community events; growth; scenarios; sporting events; stakeholder

Friedman, M, & Mason, D. (2004). A stakeholder approach to understanding economic development decision making: public subsidies for professional sport facilities. *Economic Development Quarterly*, **18**, 236-254.

Abstract: To analyze the politics of economic development decision making through focusing on participants and their interests, this article details a model of stakeholder analysis developed within organization studies by Mitchell et al. (1997) for use among policy makers and researchers. Demonstrating the model through the issue of subsidies for the construction of major league sports facilities, a stakeholder map is created to assess the constituent environment based on the degree to which stakeholders possess attributes of power, legitimacy, and urgency. With this map, various situational factors are assessed to demonstrate the utility of stakeholder analysis for decision makers to strategically manage constituent groups and to explain case outcomes and the manner in which policies are determined. Although the findings suggest that decision makers should focus their resources on stakeholders possessing all three attributes, monitoring the environment is essential to identify potential threats and opportunities.

Keywords: stakeholder analysis; stadiums; urban development

5.4.5 Media

The following diagram is adapted from the Getz and Fairley (2004) article which examined media management for a major sporting event. All the stakeholders in the diagram had important roles to play in promoting and/or covering the event. Event organizers took a very pro-active approach to ensuring that media personnel had the destination stories they needed, plus access to the stars (auto drivers) plus a good time in the Gold Coast of Australia. Knott, Fyall & Jones (2015) in their study identify the major branding opportunities for nations (beyond short-term perception changes, publicity or brand awareness) during major sport events, in this case the 2010 FIFA World Cup in South Africa. The sport event can assist destination to form a new brand image which can assist the destinations competitiveness.

Figure 5.3: Major stakeholders in sport event media management for the purpose of destination promotion. Source: Adapted from Getz and Fairley (2004)

Research note

Getz, D. & Fairley, S. (2004). Media management at sport events for destination promotion: Case studies and concepts. *Event Management*, 8, 127–139.

Abstract: The imputed links between media coverage of sport events and induced demand for host cities and destinations are discussed. Because it is so difficult to prove a causal link between media coverage and new demand, attention to improving media management of events is warranted. In this research case studies of media management for sport events in Gold Coast, Australia, were employed to assess stakeholder collaboration and media management methods. Practical implications are derived, and concepts are advanced for improved media management. In particular, the need for, and methods of, coordinated co-branding of events and destinations are examined. Research needs and priorities are identified, with specific reference to a hypothetical consumer decision-making model.

Keywords: Sport events, media management, destination promotion, image making, co-branding, Gold Coast, Australia

Knott, B., Fyall, A. & Jones, I. (2015). The nation branding opportunities provided by a sport mega-event: South Africa and the 2010 FIFA World Cup. *Journal of Destination Marketing & Management*, **4**(1), 46-56.

Abstract: Over the past decade there has been a growing awareness of the significant impact that hosting sport mega-events can have on a nations brand. This paper discusses the context of nation branding and the role of sport mega-events in generating a nation-branding legacy. A nation brand is not owned or controlled by a single organisation, but rather jointly developed and delivered by a network of public and private sector organisations. The examination of both event and brand stakeholder perceptions and experiences post the event was therefore identified as an important research area. The case of South Africa and the 2010 FIFA World Cup was selected as improving the brand image was clearly stated as an aim for the host nation. The paper is based on a qualitative study that featured in-depth interviews conducted with definitive stakeholders from the public and private sectors (n=8), within two of the major host cities of Johannesburg and Cape Town that took place two years post the event. The paper details the perceptions, experiences and reflections of these stakeholders relating to the branding opportunities and the legacy from the event and the degree to which these were leveraged. The paper contends that there are significant branding opportunities for nations beyond merely publicity, brand awareness and short-term perception changes. Greater knowledge and understanding of a brand can be developed through the experiences and engagement of visitors, citizens and members of the international business community, leading to the establishment of a more authentic brand image. Furthermore, there is also the opportunity to use these new image perceptions to position the nation brand for competitive advantage in tourism as well as business and investment sectors. Two key influencing factors of the nation branding legacy were identified, namely the media (including traditional and new media) and the role of local citizens. The discourse surrounding leveraging of legacies is furthered and supported, as it is clear that the success and legacy of the mega-event are a result of strategic activities of stakeholders. A nation branding legacy is therefore a combination of the opportunities provided by the sport mega-event and the strategic intention and activities of stakeholders.

Keywords: Nation branding, sport mega-event, 2010 FIFA World Cup, stakeholders, legacy

5.4.6 Athletes

Athletes can assist event organizers from one year to another with the design of the sport event. In the study of Fotiadis, Vassiliadis & Sotiriadis (2016) athletes were asked their specific preferences for a cycling event and they identified the season, the entertainment and awards, and parallel organized exhibitions and trades shows as some of their preferences. Event organizers also need to understand the motivational factors of athletes when planning the event and which attributes they will consider before participating. According to Ramchandani, Coleman & Bingham (2017) sport participation strategies should be built into the event planning phase. Fotiadis, Xie, Li & Huan (2016) found that travel motives, decision factors and involvement are some of these motivational factors. Research on event travel careers has revealed the event and destination preferences of highly-involved versus lesser-involved amateur athletes (e.g., Buning and Gibson, 2015 and 2016).

Research note

Fotiadis, A., Xie, L., Li, Y., & Huan, T. C. T. (2016). Attracting athletes to small-scale sports events using motivational decision-making factors. *Journal of Business Research*, **69**(11), 5467-5472.

Abstract: This study proposes and tests a model related to small-scale sport events using a conceptual model and a survey of athletes who participate in sporting events analyzed using structural equation modeling and fuzzy-set qualitative comparative analysis (fsQCA). The fsQCA results yield three models implying that small-scale event participants require a combination of attributes to consider or eventually participate. The SEM findings reveal that involvement, travel motives, and decision factors significantly affect motivational factors, and motivational factors significantly affect decision factors. A combination of positive motivation factors, positive involvement, and negative travel motives can significantly influence decision factors.

Keywords: Motivation, involvement, decision factors, sport event, fuzzy-set qualitative comparative analysis

Ramchandani, G., Coleman, R. J., & Bingham, J. (2017). Sport participation behaviours of spectators attending major sports events and event induced attitudinal changes towards sport. *International Journal of Event and Festival Management*, **8**(2), 121-135.

Abstract: *Purpose*: Evidence of the link between major sports events and increased participation at grassroots level is somewhat mixed. The purpose of this paper is to examine attitudinal changes to sport participation among spectators associated with seven sports events held in Great Britain in 2014.

Design/methodology/approach: Primary data were gathered from 4,590 spectators aged 16 and over who attended one of the events. Both positive (inspiration)

effects and negative (discouragement) effects were considered through the lens of the transtheoretical model (TTM).

Findings: The evidence from this research indicates that event audiences belong primarily to the latter (more active) stages of the TTM. It was also found that attending sports events can further fuel the existing desire of contemplators to increase participation, whereas the catalytic effect among pre-contemplators is arguably less potent. Virtually no discouragement effects were observed across the different TTM stages.

Research limitations/implications: The research stops short of measuring actual changes in sport participation post-event of individuals in the different TTM stages and any attribution of such behaviour changes to events. This is both a limitation of the current research and a natural direction for future research.

Practical implications: The main implications for promoting sport participation through the medium of sports events include attracting more people in the early stages of the TTM, greater collaboration between different event stakeholders and the building of sport participation strategies into the event planning phase.

Originality/value: Models of behaviour change such as the TTM have seldom been applied to document the current and/or planned sport participation behaviour of individuals in a sport event context or to examine attitudinal changes towards sport as a result of attending an event. An adapted version of the TTM has been proposed to overcome the limitations of the traditional model.

Keywords: Transtheoretical model, sport participation, major events

5.4.7 Funders/sponsor

Turco (2015) states that almost 70% of all sponsorship money is spent on sports. The objectives of many sport events are not to make money but they should at least be financially viable. Many of the mega sport events like the FIFA World Cup and the Olympic games are never financially viable and their focus is more on building the image of the destination. Government or corporate sponsorships can fund sport events. The event organizer wants to break even but the event sponsor or funder also would like to see some return on investment or leverage (Mackellar, 2015).

Sport managers need to examine the perception of their consumers towards sponsor characteristics before they decide who they would like the sponsor to be (Ko, Chang, Park & Herbst, 2017). Another factor to consider is the visual and cognitive process of sponsorship. (Close, Lacey & Cornwell, 2015). Scheinbaum & Lacey (2015) have found in their study that when companies sponsor community-based events it provides the organization the opportunity to demonstrate their CSR.

Research note

Mackellar, J. (2015). Determinants of business engagement with regional sport events. *European Sport Management Quarterly*, **15**(1), 7-26.

Abstract: Research question: Small-scale sports events provide commercial opportunities for regional communities, and yet research suggests that local commercial organisations are sometimes reticent to engage with sport event organisations to leverage benefits. This paper examines variation in business engagement with sport events and identifies determinants to sport event leverage that are previously unrecognised in the academic literature. Research methods: Using a multiple case study approach in three regions of eastern Australia, this research examines reactions to a sport event within each respective host business community. The multiple cases allow comparison of results across regions, using a mixed method strategy of personal interviews, observation and document analysis. Results and findings: The main findings reveal six key determinants of organisational engagement with regional sport events being: event cooperation, tourism dependency, business size, promotional strategy, strategic direction and skills and knowledge. These key determinants are explored to create a framework for future research in this area, and further contribute to the field of sport leverage research, with particular importance to sport events. Implications: The barriers to the development of strategies to maximise event leverage are identified and discussed, and in so doing implications for improving business relationships with sport events are explored. These implications are relevant to managing impacts upon businesses, visitors, and event and regional destinations.

Keywords: business engagement, sport, event, sponsorship, leverage

Scheinbaum, A. C., & Lacey, R. (2015). Event social responsibility: A note to improve outcomes for sponsors and events. *Journal of Business Research*, **68**(9), 1982-1986.

Abstract: Via a field study (n = 879), the authors introduce the concept of event social responsibility (ESR) and show how it is a catalyst for key outcomes in the business of sport. Specifically, event social responsibility leads to fan attachment to an event, event word-of-mouth, and sponsorship patronage. Fan attachment lifts consumer promotion of an event to others and mediates the relationship between ESR and the extent to which attendees share favorable WOM about the sponsored event. Results also confirm the strong link between ESR and attendees' support for sponsors, via patronage of their products. For corporate sponsors, the results offer evidence for how sponsorship of community-based events provides an opportunity for a company to demonstrate good corporate citizenship while lifting patronage intent of attendees at a professional sporting event.

Keywords: Experiential marketing, event marketing effectiveness, sponsorship, corporate social responsibility, business of sport

5.4.8 Supporters

All stakeholders in the destination need to work together and support a sport event for it to be successful. Taks at el. (2018) in their research on the International Children's Games found that there was distrust among the sport clubs locally and the event organizers. The objectives and goals of these stakeholders with the event differ and had a negative impact on the outcome of the event. The buy-in of government is always important in hosting sport events as offering these events might need a change in local laws and regulations. Quatar was awarded the 2022 FIFA World Cup finals and according to Brannagan & Rookwood (2016) some domestic policies might need to be changed.

Research note

Taks, M., Green, B. C., Misener, L. & Chalip, L. (2018). Sport participation from sport events: why it doesn't happen. *Marketing Intelligence & Planning*, **36**(2), 185-198.

Abstract: *Purpose*: The purpose of this paper is to present and use an event leveraging framework (ELF) to examine processes and challenges when seeking to leverage a sport event to build sport participation.

Design/methodology/approach: The study used an action research approach for which the researchers served as consultants and facilitators for local sports in the context of the International Children's Games. Initially three sports were selected, and two sports were guided through the full leveraging process. Prior to the event, actions were planned and refined, while researchers kept field notes. Challenges and barriers to implementation were examined through observation immediately prior to and during the event, and through a workshop with stakeholders six weeks after the event, and interviews a year later.

Findings: With the exception of a flyer posted on a few cars during the track and field competition, none of the planned action steps was implemented. Barriers included competition and distrust among local sport clubs, exigencies associated with organizing event competitions, the event organizers' focus on promoting the city rather than its sports, and each club's insufficient human and physical resources for the task. These barriers were not addressed by local clubs because they expected the event to inspire participation despite their lack of marketing leverage. The lack of action resulted in no discernible impact of the event on sport participation.

Research limitations/implications: Results demonstrate that there are multiple barriers to undertaking the necessary steps to capitalize on an event to build sport participation, even when a well-developed framework is used. Specific steps to overcome the barriers need to be implemented, particularly through partnerships and building capacity for leverage among local sport organizations.

Originality/value: This study presents the ELF, and identifies reasons why sport events fail to live up to their promise to build sport participation. Necessary steps are suggested to redress that failing.

Keywords: Evaluation, Outcomes, Organizational capacity, Event leverage, Sport clubs, Sport organizations

Brannagan, P. M., & Rookwood, J. (2016). Sports mega-events, soft power and soft disempowerment: international supporters' perspectives on Qatar's acquisition of the 2022 FIFA World Cup finals. *International Journal of Sport Policy and Politics*, **8**(2), 173-188.

Abstract: Through the use of document analysis, field work and semi-structured interviews at five major tournaments in Asia, North America, Europe and South America, the paper examines the perspectives of international football supporters on the Fédération Internationale de Football Association's (FIFA) decision to award the 2022 World Cup finals to the State of Qatar. The paper is separated into five sections. First we ground Qatar's sporting strategy within the concept of 'soft power', as well as pinpoint the negative consequences that have manifest since the state's acquisition of the 2022 finals. Second, we disclose and defend our chosen data collection strategy. Third, we uncover and discuss our results with reference to three key themes: the state's suitability as a football destination; the dubious awarding of the 2022 World Cup; and, Qatar's cultural backdrop and domestic policies. Fourth, we align our findings to Qatar's foreign policy intentions and 'soft disempowerment' consequences, locating in the process the opportunities and challenges that accompany the state's hosting of the 2022 finals. We conclude by reflecting upon the contribution we have made here, as well as acknowledging the importance of Qatar for current and future sports mega-event research.

Keywords: Qatar, soft power, global sport, football, sports fandom, sports corruption

5.4.9 Spectators

Spectators can influence the way in which certain sports are being managed. In Numerato's (2015) study the criticism of football spectators against modern football is being investigated and the outcome of dissatisfied spectators led to protest and reflexive discursive practices. Horbel et al. (2016) applied the service dominant logic, specifically value co-creation, to see how sport event organizers can evaluate experience and successfully facilitate value co-creation and make meaning full propositions to the benefit of all involved.

Research note

Numerato, D. (2015). Who says 'no' to modern football? Italian supporters, reflexivity, and neo-liberalism. *Journal of Sport and Social Issues*, **39**(2), 120-138.

Abstract: This study explores the complexities and ambiguities of the recent increase in criticism among football supporters of so-called "modern football." Drawing on existing elaborations of the concept of reflexivity in sociology, this contribution theoretically extends the hegemony/resistance analytical framework that has commonly been used to portray the criticism of football supporters in strict opposition to neo-liberal trends. The examination of the social and symbolic mechanisms surrounding anti-neo-liberal campaigning suggests that the slogan has been embraced by heterogeneous actors with contrasting topics, values, beliefs, and opinions. Considering the different reactions of contested anti-neo-liberal institutions and the context in which these processes take place, it has been demonstrated that protests and reflexive discursive practices can both inhibit and enhance the transformative potential of the "Against modern football" slogan.

Keywords: emotions, neo-liberalism, reflexivity, resistance, football supporters

Horbel, C., Popp, B., Woratschek, H., & Wilson, B. (2016). How context shapes value co-creation: spectator experience of sport events. *The Service Industries Journal*, **36**(11-12), 510-531.

Abstract: This paper applies the perspective of service-dominant logic, specifically value co-creation in service ecosystems to the context of sports. It builds on the notion that co-created value can only be understood as value-in-context. Therefore, a structural model is developed and tested for different contexts of spectating live broadcasts of football games during the Fédération Internationale de Football Association World Cup 2014. The context-specific contributions of the co-creating actors, spectators' experience evaluations, and the resulting context-specific value perceptions from the spectators' perspective are identified. The results highlight that the relative influence of the main co-creating actors and the relative importance of the value dimensions differ across contexts. Service providers (in sports) should identify how consumers evaluate experience and which dimensions of value are most important to them in the context under consideration. This will help them to successfully facilitate value co-creation, make meaningful value propositions, and achieve strategic benefit for themselves.

Keywords: Service-dominant logic, service ecosystems, value-in-context, sport event experience, value co-creation

5.5 Stakeholder management for business events

Sometimes this category is referred to as the MICE sector, that is Meetings, Incentives, Conventions (or Conferences) and Exhibitions. It also includes fairs and trade shows, international congresses and any other type of event devoted to business or marketing.

Meetings and conventions are different for associations and private businesses. The corporate sector, in addition to its internal routine meetings, holds public relations and events and engages in 'live communications' through event sponsorship. Some corporations own their events, for branding or sales purposes. Associations are voluntary organizations representing the interests of members, and they hold numerous meetings and conventions. At conventions delegates vote for their leaders. The events of corporations and associations are important to convention centers and other venues, so much so that permanent relationships are sought with meeting planners. Decisions to locate in a particular city or venue might be based on direct sales or competitive bidding.

There are big differences between trade and consumer shows. Industry sectors have their own shows for Business to Business networking, and sometimes these are combined with consumer shows for the people interested in, say, cars, recreation, health or the latest electronic gadgetry. An interesting combination as identified by Mackellar (2006) is how a convention, a festival and the tourism organization can work together and use an agricultural convention in conjunction with a festival to attract more people and also to share resources. A network analysis was utilized to understand the all the industry relationships. Morla & Ladkin (2006) research looks at the successes and potential growth of the convention industry in Santiago de Compostela and Galicia by taking a stakeholder perspective and by asking their stakeholders to identify some areas of growth.

Research note

Mackellar, J. (2006). Conventions, festivals, and tourism: Exploring the network that binds. *Journal of Convention and Event Tourism*, **8** (2), 45-56.

Abstract: The link between conventions and tourism has often been assumed, and to some extent has been researched, and yet little research has been undertaken to study the relationships between organizations staging an event. The aim of this paper is to highlight the links between convention, festival, and tourism organizations using a case study in Lismore, Australia. The Lismore Chamber of Commerce has used an agricultural convention in conjunction with a community festival to share resources and attract wider audiences. This paper demonstrates the outcomes of this relationship in terms of innovation, cooperation, and regional development. Where previous attempts to coordinate the herb industry had failed, the case shows how coordinated events can serve an important purpose. The case also demonstrates the use of a network analysis methodology as a potential tool for researchers and managers in identifying and understanding industry relationships. The results demonstrate the success of this event and highlight the importance of developing and maintaining network relations.

Keywords: Conventions, festivals, tourism organizations, resources, network analysis methodology, network relations

Morla, D. & Ladkin, A. (2006). The convention industry in Galicia and Santiago de Compostela: Stakeholder perceptions of its success and potential for growth. *Event Management,* **10** (4), 241-251.

Abstract: The Autonomous Community of Galicia, Spain and its regional capital city Santiago de Compostela have a well-developed and successful convention industry. This research outlines the reasons for its success, and, taking a stakeholder perspective, explores ways in which the region can ensure continued growth. Using primary data based on interviews with different stakeholders from the public and private sectors, a number of issues are examined in relation to potential for growth. These include the current perceptions of the destination's success, the role of the conference and exhibition centers and promotion of the destination, increasing competition, and human resources. The study concludes with recommendations for improvements for the Galician convention industry, and a discussion of how these issues might be relevant for other convention destinations.

Keywords: Conventions, Galicia, potential growth, stakeholder perceptions

5.6 Stakeholder management for festivals

Festivals sometimes develop organically from within communities, or at least require strong community support to endure; so comprehensive management of stakeholders is critical. Derrett (2016) in the book *The Complete Guide to Creating Enduring Festivals* devoted a chapter to partnerships. Her view (p. 96) is that festivals cannot be viewed simply as providing a service to a target market, but that they are "...just one part of a mosaic that satisfies diverse stakeholders...". In creating an enduring "festival ecosystem" stakeholder management for festivals will place the customer at the center and then seek mutual benefit from all the partnerships needed to implement strategy. Derret's "partnership components" include consultation, commitment, context, content, collaboration and cooperation, communication, creativity and innovation, contracts and controls, conflict resolution, competitors, customers, community engagement, economy, contribution, corporate and social responsibility, and consequences. There is clearly a long list of C-words to remember! As to festival stakeholder roles, Derrett provided a comprehensive list. For example, roles for sponsors and co-producers include demonstrating local corporate goodwill, sharing target markets, establishing links to host destination, sharing brand, and naming rights.

Festival stakeholders also have different motivations to participate in local festivals (Adongo & Kim, 2018). Adongo (2017) looked from a multiple dyadic relationship at how festival stakeholders interact with each other and the strategies they use to collaborate. They also compare the views on the stakeholder exchanges between them based on control and dependence, trust, altruism and reciprocity. In some cases there are not much tension between stakeholders although it can happen (Vilas & Wada, 2017) and in other areas the interaction between festival organizers, residents and local businesses help drive entrepreneurial activities during festivals (Hjalager & Kwiatkowski, 2017). The sustainability of festivals is also often dependent on the tangible support of key stakeholders (Andersson & Getz, 2008) and engagement between stakeholders and stakeholder benefits and desbenefits must yet to be researched (Carlsen, Ali-Knight & Robertson, 2007).

Research note

Adongo, R. & Kim, S. (2018). The ties that bind: stakeholder collaboration and networking in local festivals. *International Journal of Contemporary Hospitality Management*, **30**(6), 2458-2480

Abstract: *Purpose*: This study aims to examine the extent of collaboration and networking between local festival stakeholders by focusing on the differences in how they evaluate themselves and other stakeholders.

Design/methodology/approach: A questionnaire directed toward different stakeholder groups involving 1,092 respondents was administered at six selected festivals in Ghana, West Africa.

Findings: In terms of self-evaluated collaboration and networking, the festival organizers considered themselves to have the highest risk, followed by the sponsors and vendors. However, when the stakeholders assessed each other, most agreed that they experienced higher risk when dealing with vendors. To reduce the risks of dealing with vendors, it is recommended that vendors be registered, accredited and allocated selling spaces before festivals begin.

Practical implications: It is helpful to understand the nature of decision power or different views of collaboration and networking among stakeholders. Further, this study offers insights to understand stakeholders' motivations to participate in local festivals.

Originality/value: - The combination of collaboration and networking between local festival stakeholders into a conceptual model allows the current findings to offer meaningful theoretical and practical implications.

Keywords: Festivals, collaboration, stakeholders, networking

Vilkas, Á., & Wada, E. (2017). Hospitality and stakeholders in events. Multiple case study in Florianópolis, Santa Catarina, Brazil. *Revista Turismo & Desenvolvimento*, **27/28** (1), 217-228.

Abstract : The approach of this research was to understand the hospitality relations between the stakeholdersstakeholders and the organizers of Carnaval, Réveillon, Fenaostra, Boi-de-Mamão and Festa do Divino, in Florianópolis, Santa Catarina. The city of Florianopolis is visited by tourists seeking sun and beach, and seasonality outside the summer period, so that the events that happen in high season receive more tourists compared to smaller events that happen another seasons. To understand this scene and achieve the research goal, which was to identify the stakeholders of each event, the research was conducted by a multiple case study (Yin, 2010), and participant observation. There were in-depth interviews based on semi-structured script with the events organizers, and with stakeholders nominated by them. The results were analysed using the methods of Bardin (2011). They show that stakeholders don't have tensions between them, but it can happen; the big events have as many stakeholders as smaller or traditional events; the hospitality between the stakeholders contributes to the growth of tourism.

Andersson, T. & Getz, D. (2008). Stakeholder management strategies of festivals. In *Journal of Convention & Event Tourism*, **9**(3), 199-220.

Abstract: The extent to which festivals can function as sustainable attractions, while fulfilling their social and cultural roles at the community level, is an issue of considerable importance. In this context, sustainability will often depend upon the political and tangible support of key stakeholders. Accordingly, this article addresses festival stakeholder issues and related management strategies, with the dual aims of contributing to event management theory and improving festival viability. A questionnaire survey of 14 live-music festivals in Sweden yielded data on stakeholder types, dependency issues, and stakeholder management strategies. With regard to their long-term sustainability, festival managers indicated the importance of attaining 'institutional status,' occupying a unique 'niche' in the community, sustaining committed stakeholders, and practicing constant innovation.

Keywords. Festivals, stakeholders, dependency, strategy, institutions, Sweden

Carlsen, J., Ali-Knight, J. & Robertson, M. (2007). Access—a research agenda for Edinburgh festivals. *Event Management*, **11**(1-2), 3-11.

Abstract: Festivals and events have assumed a prominent place in the social and economic fabric of Edinburgh, to a point where it now enjoys a reputation as a leading festival and event destination. In Edinburgh, as in other festival destinations, most of the research and evaluation effort has been concerned with 'proving' the economic benefits of individual events. The limitations of focusing on narrow economic outcomes are now widely recognized in terms of the comparability, reliability, and utility of the estimates produced. While the attention of stakeholders has been on economic benefits, the very important cultural, community, and social benefits have been overlooked. Important issues such as engagement with the arts, community, cultural, social, and stakeholder benefits and disbenefits produced have yet to be researched in any systematic way. This article offers a comprehensive research agenda for key festivals in Edinburgh and acts an introduction to this special issue. The research agenda is based on published articles (inclusive of those in this volume), existing strategies and documentation, and the editors' knowledge of and engagement with the Edinburgh festival community. The agenda will be of interest to the numerous festivals and events stakeholders in Edinburgh as well as other destinations that are seeking to understand the social and cultural, as well the economic, dimensions of festivals.

Keywords: Cultural benefits, economic benefits, Edinburgh, events, festivals, social benefits

The relevance of Institutional Theory

Wikipedia defines an institution this way: *"Institutions are 'stable, valued, recurring patterns of behavior'. As structures or mechanisms of social order, they govern the behavior of a set of individuals within a given community. Institutions are identified with a social purpose, transcending individuals and intentions by mediating the rules that govern living behavior."*

Institutions can be social/legal constructs, like marriage or the family, or real organizations like the church or an event. Institutions generate public good, as conceived within particular cultures, solving important social problems or attaining valued goals. Permanence and stability are associated with institutions, so is tradition.

Few scholars have looked at events this way. Getz and Andersson (2008) found that many festival managers tended to believe they were permanent institutions in their host communities, or at least that they strived for recognition of that status. In exchange for giving up a degree of independence, events as institutions can gain permanent support.

Research note

Getz, D., & Andersson, T. (2008). Sustainable festivals: on becoming an institution. *Event Management*, **12** (1), 1-17.

Abstract: This article conceptually addresses the sustainability of festivals from the perspective of the organizations providing them, specifically in the context of how event organizations can become permanent institutions. Festivals and other recurring events are often viewed as tourist attractions, and are commonly used in place marketing and destination image-making strategies. Little attention has been paid, however, to their individual or collective viability and long-term sustainability. Supportive data are provided from a survey of 14 live-music festivals in Sweden in which responding festival managers confirmed the importance of attaining 'institutional status', occupying a unique 'niche' in the community, sustaining committed stakeholders, and practicing constant innovation. Theoretical conclusions are drawn on the institutionalization process for festivals, including a set of propositions that can be used both as indicators of institutional status, and as hypotheses for future research.

Keywords: Event organizations, festivals, institutions, stakeholders, sustainability

The political market square

Larson and Wikstrom (2001) and Larson (2002) in adapting the 'political market square' concept to events and other projects did not mention stakeholder theory, but drew from inter-organizational theory, collaboration, and project network theory. In the political market square (it is a metaphor) actors can form alliances, power is exercised, the legitimacy of actors is important (requiring trust) and gatekeepers or powerful actors might make decisions as to who participates. Collaboration and consensus building is the preferred approach, versus conflict, and this is at the heart of stakeholder theory as well.

Within a project network, or event organization, there are likely to be dynamic tensions as stakeholders come and go and vie for influence. Collaboration can come about through mutual trust and assigning legitimacy to the other stakeholders' perspectives. A process is required to deal with inevitable conflicts. Who has the most power will often be a key determinant of decision-making. These tensions are also linked to organizational culture, and that makes them political in nature.

An additional article by Larson (2009) explicitly relates to stakeholder and institutional theories, and adds to the political market square metaphor by focusing on the change process in event networks. The "jungle, the park, and the garden" describe three models, with the jungle representing a tumultuous network, the park being dynamic, and the garden suggesting a stable institution. Larson argued that an institutionalized network, say a hallmark event, runs the risk of becoming stale, whereas in a more open, and therefor dynamic environment, new actors are brought in along with new ideas.

Research notes

Larson, M. (2009). Joint event production in the jungle, the park, and the garden: Metaphors of event networks. *Tourism Management*, **30**(3), 393-399.

Abstract: This article argues that actors in different event networks experience different dynamics in terms of the joint organizing of the event. The Political Market Square (PSQ) model is used to describe, analyze and compare the interactions and dynamics going on in three event networks. The purpose is to categorize different kinds of PSQs in terms of actors' interactions and network dynamics, which, in turn, contributes to knowledge on how events are produced using a network perspective. An analysis of the different event networks resulted in three different categories of Political Market Squares – the jungle, the park, and the garden, representing a tumultuous, a dynamic, and an institutionalized event network. The institutionalized PSQ (the park) is often prescribed in literature on event organizing. Therefore, more research focused on understanding tumultuous and dynamic event networks (the jungle and the park) are needed.

Keywords: Event networks, political market square, access, interaction, change dynamics, metaphors

Getz, D., Andersson, T. & Larson, M. (2006). Festival stakeholder roles: Concepts and case studies. *Event Management*, **10**(2-3), 103-122.

Abstract: In this exploratory research, multiple case studies of various types of festivals in two countries reveal how festival managers work with stakeholders and who they are. Stakeholders' roles are categorized as regulator, facilitator, co-producer, supplier, collaborator, audience, and the impacted, and the results show clearly that key stakeholders take multiple roles affecting the organization. Practical implications are drawn for event managers regarding the identification, evaluation, and management of stakeholder relationships. Drawing on resource dependency and stakeholder theories, a conceptual model is presented that illustrates the conclusion that festivals and events are produced within and by a set of managed stakeholder relationships. Recommendations are made for development of this line of research and theory building.

Keywords: Festival management, Stakeholder theory, Network theory, Resource dependency, Calgary, Canada, Sweden

5.7 Stakeholder management for mega events

The bigger the event the greater the challenge – it seems obvious. But are the stakeholder roles and relationships categorically different from those experienced by small events? Are the management strategies inherently different? There is a huge body of literature on the Olympics, so much so that it can be considered a sub-field on its own. Also covered by many researchers and commentators have been the World Cup of football/soccer and other international sport events, and World's Fairs or Expos.

Organizing the Olympic Games is a complex task (Gargalianos, Toohey & Stotlar, 2015) and involves a multitude of individuals and stakeholders (Frawley, 2015). As previously mentioned the local community plays a very important role as stakeholders of mega events (Sadd, 2012).

Research notes

Frawley, S. (2015). Organizational Power and the management of a mega-event: the case of Sydney 2000. *Event Management*, **19** (2), 247-260.

Abstract: The organization of a mega-event such as the Olympic Games is a complex task involving a multitude of individuals and stakeholder groups. In 2000, Australia's largest city, Sydney, staged the Summer Olympic Games. The agency given primary responsibility for these Games was the Sydney Organizing Committee for the Olympic Games (SOCOG). Two additional organizations also played a central role in the management of the event: The Australian Olympic Committee and the New South Wales Government. This article explores the role played by the host national Olympic committee as a key Olympic stakeholder in the organization of the Olympic Games. The research highlights that organization of a mega-project, such as the Olympic Games, is not only the result of recent developments but also of countless social and organizational figurations that developed over many years prior to the winning of a bid to stage the event.

Keywords: Mega-events, Olympic games, organizational power, stakeholder management

Gargalianos, D., Toohey, K. & Stotlar, D. (2015). Olympic Games Complexity Model (Ogcm). *Event Management*, **19**, 47–55

Abstract: The Olympic Games (OG) is a complex event project. This conceptual article aims at presenting the complexity of the Games by virtue of a three-dimensional, graphic model depicting the event's stakeholders and the interrelationships among them from the perspective of an Organizing Committee for the Olympic Games (OCOG). The model evolved from: a) content analysis of relevant literature (i.e., IOC organizational documents regarding the OCOG) and b) personal participation and observation of the authors in the organization of the Games. The model allows managers of OCOGs, especially those who do not have previous experience in Olympic matters, to quickly and comprehensively understand the complex and entwined organizational processes, as well the various stakeholder relationships that may not at first be readily apparent.

Keywords: Olympic Games, complexity, stakeholders

Sadd, D. (2010). What is event-led regeneration? Are we confusing terminology or will London 2012 be the first games to truly benefit the local existing population? *Event Management*, **13**, 265–275.

Abstract: When London won the bid to host the Games, the vision was underpinned by key themes, one of which was to leave a legacy of benefiting the community through regeneration. The regeneration of the Lower Lea Valley was promised to be for the direct benefit of everyone who lives and works there, involving significant social and economic advancement. However, Mace, Hall, and Gallent draw parallels through the previous urban regeneration projects in major cities and they argue that for regeneration to work it has to be for the benefit of the existing communities and not 'new' communities who inhabit the area post the Games. Could this happen in East London and, despite Government plans, the developments lead to an extension of the Docklands renaissance, inhabited instead by mostly middle class workers? This article explores the difference between regeneration and gentrification in the context of London 2012 and other Olympic Games. Much of the published literature regarding London's legacy of urban regeneration has a positive slant, yet, through the analysis of documentation from previous Games and through in-depth interviews with key stakeholders, the research highlights a number of issues that London 2012 will need to address.

Keywords: Regeneration, event legacies, London 2012, gentrification, community as stakeholder

5.8 Case study: 2010 FIFA World Cup, Potchefstroom, South Africa

Elmarie Slabbert – North West University – South Africa

Jacques F Faul – Titans Cricket – South Africa

Soccer World Cup 2010 – Base camp city stakeholders

Mega sporting events create huge public interest and are reported to a world audience. South Africa's hosting of the 2010 FIFA World Cup was no exception. The FIFA World Cup, per viewership, is regarded as one of the largest sporting events in the world. The announcement that South Africa had won the bid to host the event in 2010 was made in May 2004, consisting of 32 teams playing 64 matches over 200 viewing hours at ten stadia (in nine cities). This was the first time that Africa would host a mega sports event and there was some comments concerning South Africa's ability to make a success of this event. The tournament was hosted by nine cities and was served by 32 base camps in 2010.

A base camp is defined as a place to work, rest and play. It should be the perfect place for tournament preparation. Potchefstroom (in the North-West Province) was one of two base camp cities that was not a hosting city. However, being a base camp city still requires preparation, infrastructure development, community interaction and marketing campaigns. Stakeholder management is carefully planned for hosting cities to ensure the optimisation of benefits, but the same does not necessarily apply to base-camp cities. However, the same benefit expectations are created in base camp cities in the planning of these events. Unfortunately, these benefits are seldom realised, thus leaving the base camp city with very few benefits for being part of the mega event.

To be selected as a base camp city it is important to have quality accommodation and training facilities and the altitude could be a factor. It is also important for a base camp city to have leisure and entertainment options available for the players and keep the travel distances short. A controlled and secure environment that stimulates the competition conditions as closely as possible is required from a base camp. Thus cities bidding to be a base camp must assess whether the requirements are in place before embarking on the responsibility which involves a number of stakeholders.

Different stakeholders for the event

A number of stakeholders are involved in the bidding for and being a base camp city to be discussed on two levels.

Level one stakeholders

♦ *National federation:* This organization has a number of rules that need to be adhered to in bidding to be a base camp city.

♦ *Potchefstroom local organizing committee:* This committee consists of a number of people with interest in serving as a base camp city and taking responsibility for the bidding and hosting.

Level two stakeholders

♦ *Host community businesses:* Businesses that would benefit directly or indirectly from an influx of visitors to the city or from the team itself are important role players and include businesses such as restaurants, accommodation, tourism attractions, etc.

♦ *Host community residents*: The local community plays a critical role in serving as a welcome host to the participating team. They have certain expectations of the city being a base camp city.

♦ *Tourism and hospitality establishments:* These should benefit directly from an influx of sports spectators and those following certain teams to where they train and prepare for the tournament.

♦ *Media*: Journalists play a critical role in the reporting of sporting events and in the case of a mega sports event the information is shared with the world.

♦ *Team management:* This includes everyone involved in the team which includes management, players, athletes, conditioning staff and coaches. They are considered a key stakeholder since teams showcase the sport and participate.

♦ *Base camp accommodation*: The establishments provide accommodation directly to the team and are actively involved in the bidding process as a base-camp city.

♦ *Base camp training venues:* These venues are critical in securing a base camp city as the training venues should offer state-of-the-art equipment and staff to serve the needs of these international teams for six weeks.

♦ *Local government*: This stakeholder plays a critical role in the bidding for and hosting of the team as a base camp city due to their role in development, provision of infrastructure and services as well as financial support.

The process followed to identify the stakeholders

The local organising committee of Potchefstroom took responsibility in developing the bid for this city to be a base camp city. The North-West University took the lead in identifying the different stakeholders and meeting with identified parties to get buy-in in the event and serving as a host city. Being a base camp city was considered a marketing tool that can hold significant benefits for Potchefstroom.

The importance of stakeholders

All the mentioned stakeholders are important in different phases of this event. Some are more important before the event and others during and after the event. However, there are two stakeholders that were significantly more important for the reasons provided below.

The national federation was a very important stakeholder as they had to be convinced that Potchefstroom adheres to the requirements of being a base camp city and they needed to award this bid to the city. To do this presentation, the local organising committee had to do careful planning, involve various stakeholders and put the final bid together.

However, the most important stakeholder group was the team management of the soccer teams. These teams have specific requirements regarding accommodation, training facilities, food, leisure facilities, management of fans and transport. If they are not satisfied with the products and services provided, they consider a different location.

Involvement of stakeholders

The local organising committee consisted of representatives from the different stakeholder groups which allowed for access to these groups. In general, the local public and other stakeholders were informed of the possible benefits and outcomes of being a base camp city using local media and face-to-face meetings. Promises were made on the number of tourists that will follow the team staying in Potchefstroom which created enthusiasm for serving as a base camp city. One of the requirements of the Spain team was the upgrade of the airstrip which was done and it was also necessary to build accommodation for the team which is currently known as the Sports Village. To a great extent, the involvement of the stakeholders was a concerted effort with high hopes for the event.

Problems with the stakeholders

The effort to bid as a base camp city led to stakeholders working together in Potchefstroom before the event. However, with the changing global economic conditions in 2010 fewer tourists came to South Africa to participate in the tournament. This changed the attitudes of certain stakeholders since few additional visitors followed the Spain team to Potchefstroom. The promises of additional economic income did not materialize and a number of stakeholders were furious about the money lost due to that. This will influence future participation of these stakeholders in similar events.

Specific focus on the local community

Being a base camp city did not directly involved all residents, but it created a sense of pride to be hosting an international sports team (also the winning team in the end) locally. The local community was informed of the arrival of the Spain team and residents took to the streets to welcome the team to Potchefstroom. The local newspaper also indicated which training sessions could be attended by the residents and some of the information signs were changed into Spanish. Some local businesses changed their facilities and bought additional stock, but the outcome was not as expected.

Management of the stakeholders

The local organising committee was responsible for the management of the stakeholders, especially those with direct involvement in the base camp location. To a certain extent this was challenging since each group (persons in some cases) had their own agenda. In many cases, governments utilize these types of events to gain political favour from the voters and it was not different in the case of Potchefstroom. It is necessary to develop a power/interest grid to define the role of stakeholders forming part of a base camp city and not necessarily serving as a hosting city.

Lessons learned from the stakeholder engagement

♦ Never underestimate the agendas and motivation of different stakeholder groups

♦ External influences, such as recession, can change the whole outlook of stakeholders and with that their attitudes and willingness to participate in future events

♦ The overall 'feel-good' effect created by serving as hosts for the winning team still affects today where the community is proud of their input.

♦ Not all stakeholder groups benefit equally from a mega sporting event.

5.9 Stakeholder management for hallmark events

When events become permanent institutions, co-branded with their city or destination, we can call them 'hallmark events' (the term 'signature event' is sometimes used). They are usually old, large, and considered to be (or to embody) traditions. As institutions, they solve important social problems or satisfy a range of community goals and benefits (Nordvall & Heldt, 2017), from culture to tourism (Todd, Leask & Ensor, 2017) and legacy projects (Beek & Go, 2017). And they are place dependent, meaning they cannot be moved or separated from their environment without losing their inherent appeal. If a hallmark event fails, or is at risk, there will be a public outcry and a political will to save it. All of this implies they have worked out their stakeholder relationship for mutual benefit, have solved problems or survived crises, and have become resilient.

Research notes

Todd, L., Leask, A., & Ensor, J. (2017). Understanding primary stakeholders' multiple roles in hallmark event tourism management. *Tourism Management*, **59**, 494-509.

Abstract: This paper contributes insights into stakeholder theory in hallmark event tourism and the implications for engaging primary stakeholders in further tourism management settings. The tangible and symbolic tourism benefits instilled in destinations by hallmark events are well-documented; with destination managers increasingly adopting event portfolio approaches to nurture and develop existing and new hallmark events. Nevertheless, limited understanding exists of how stakeholders engage with hallmark events over time; their lived experiences in event tourism; and consequent management implications. This paper uncovers multiple and shifting roles of primary stakeholders in a long-established hallmark event tourism context (Edinburgh's Festival Fringe). It presents a typology identifying five primary stakeholder roles. Phenomenological interviews with twenty-one primary stakeholders revealed that most fulfilled multiple roles. Existing concurrently and historically, these differed throughout stakeholders' lived experiences and engagement. In its findings, this paper extends knowledge of stakeholders' roles in event tourism and implications in further tourism management settings.

Keywords: Stakeholders, multiple roles, hallmark event tourism, lived experience

Beek, R. & Go F. (2017). Legacy of hallmark events: Cross-cultural analysis among emerging destinations. In: Little, S., Go, F. and Poon, T.C. (eds), *Global Innovation and Entrepreneurship: Challenges and Experiences from East and West* (pp. 273–314). Cham, Switzerland: Palgrave Macmillan.

Abstract: Destinations strive to host international hallmark events like the Olympic Games and FIFA World Cup™ to create a positive legacy. Hallmark events influence multiple domains of legacy (e.g. economic, infrastructural, social, and political) that vary in terms of tonality, tangibility, and sustainability. Recent hallmark events as well as international hallmark events in the upcoming decade will be mainly hosted by emerging destinations, including Brazil, Russia, India, China, and South Africa (BRICSA). Which tendencies and dilemmas can be identified when comparing the legacy of hallmark events hosted in these so-called BRICSA destinations? Cross-cultural dynamics are of importance in such a multiple case study among different destinations and different hallmark events (Preuss & Alfs, 2007). This chapter contributes to the understanding of the heterogeneous effects of hosting hallmark events in emerging destinations in order to, first, support decision makers in their judgment about the organization of such comprehensive projects. Second, this chapter provides a research agenda to indicate relevant gaps in the understandings of the legacy of hallmark events, especially when related to the context of emerging destinations. Third, as methodology lacks to draw tendencies based on the conclusions of previous investigations of hallmark event legacy, this chapter aims to indicate research approaches for comparative multiple case studies.

Keywords: Olympic Games, sport event, multiple case study, stakeholder dialogue, destination image.

Nordvall, A., & Heldt, T. (2017). Understanding hallmark event failure: a case study of a Swedish music festival. *International Journal of Event and Festival Management*, 8(2), 172-185.

Abstract: *Purpose*: Hallmark events can be very beneficial for host communities, not least due to their potential in attracting tourists. The Peace & Love music festival was the hallmark event of the Swedish city Borlänge. In 2013, the event organization declared bankruptcy and canceled the forthcoming festival. The purpose of this paper is to identify and discuss the factors that caused the failure of the 2013 Peace & Love festival.

Design/methodology/approach: The case of the Peace & Love festival is analyzed using three data sources: interviews with the former members of the event organization; secondary data describing the Swedish festival industry; and festival visitors' perspectives represented by comments on social media. An organizational ecology perspective frames the analysis.

Findings: The results of the study reveal that the failure of the event can be understood by a combination of three components: an organization in a vulnerable position, a strong new competitor entering the Swedish festival market, and uncertain visitors searching for the new place to be.

Originality/value: Very few studies have researched event failure, although the subject is a recommended priority within the field of festival studies. This study presents a thorough examination of a hallmark event failure, which contributes to this area of knowledge and provides relevant information for organizations and host cities.

Keywords: Event failure, Festival industry, Festival organization, Hallmark event, Organizational ecology, Festival visitors' behaviour

The classic reference is from Ritchie and Beliveau (1974) who studied the Quebec Winter Carnival and coined the term 'hallmark event' to describe its importance in place marketing and attracting tourists. Although it focused on economic impacts, this paper described the event as an important institution within the community. The more recent paper by Getz et al. (2012) explores the concept of hallmark events in detail and describes a planning process for their creation that emphasizes community benefits and sustainability.

Research notes

Ritchie, J. B., & Beliveau, D. (1974). Hallmark events: An evaluation of a strategic response to seasonality in the travel market. *Journal of Travel Research*, **13**(2), 14-20.

Abstract: Cyclical demand in the leisure, recreation, and travel markets is a major factor contributing to low productivity and low returns on investment among the suppliers of goods and services to these markets. One strategic response to "the seasonality problem," which has had varying degrees of success in different regions, is termed the Hallmark Event. Such events, built around a major theme, serve to focus tourism and recreational planning on a particular period of the year. The present research provides both an in-depth, cross-sectional study of one such activity (The Quebec Winter Carnival) as well as a longitudinal analysis of the event's evolution over its 20-year history. Finally, the social and economic implications of the findings are discussed with a view to aiding persons interested in developing such events.

Getz, D., Svensson, B., Peterssen, R. & Gunnervall, A. (2012). Hallmark events: definition, goals and planning process. *International Journal of Event Management Research, 7*, (1/2)

Abstract: This paper defines and conceptualizes hallmark events, as there is neither clarity in the literature about what the term means nor the exact roles they should play within a community and tourism context. This generates a model for use by communities and other event-tourism developers. Our model is structured around three main outcome goals (attraction, image and branding, and the community) and three major process goals (sustainability, marketing, and organization and ownership). This paper is the first attempt to define and conceptualize a critical concept in both the event tourism and event management literature.

Keywords: Hallmark events; ontology; planning process; model

Brent Ritchie, J. R. (1984). Assessing the impact of hallmark events: Conceptual and research issues. *Journal of Travel Research*, **23**(1), 2-11.

Abstract: This article examines the numerous impacts of hallmark events on the destination area which has generated the event. These effects include not only the economic results but also the physical, socio-cultural, psychological, and political impacts such events have.

5.10   Stakeholder management for iconic events

These events have symbolic meaning to special-interest groups. Hallmark events also have symbolic meaning, so there is a possible overlap. For example, Boston Marathon is iconic in the running world and is a signature event for the city. But numerous iconic events will remain small and known only to insiders (raising the importance of Social Worlds theory). Accordingly, their primary stakeholders are members of particular social worlds or other defined special-interest groups, such as foodies, cyclist (Bull & Lovell, 2007; Berridge, 2012) amateur runners, or yoga practitioners.

Research notes

Bull, C., & Lovell, J. (2007). The impact of hosting major sporting events on local residents: An analysis of the views and perceptions of Canterbury residents in relation to the Tour de France 2007. *Journal of Sport & Tourism*, **12**(3-4), 229-248.

Abstract: While much is written on the economic and social impacts of certain types of major sports tourism event such as the Olympic Games and soccer World Cup, there has been relatively little assessment of different types of event, such as the Tour de France. Furthermore, most impact studies assess the impacts either during or after the event. This paper examines certain impacts in relation to the Tour de France Stage One race that ended in the city of Canterbury on 8 July 2007, but adopts a different approach by examining the views and perceptions of residents in the run up to the event rather than looking at impacts per se. 408 residents were interviewed to assess the extent to which the local population was aware of the event, likely to participate in it and how far they would support it. In addition, the study was also concerned to assess the effectiveness of the City Council's promotional campaign. Results showed that the vast majority of residents were aware of the event with many planning to watch the race or participate in related activities. Furthermore, despite the potential for various negative impacts, there was overwhelming support for the decision to host the event, suggesting a very successful promotional campaign by the City Council.

Keywords: Sports tourism, events, Tour de France, residents' perceptions, social and economic impacts

Berridge, G. (2012). The promotion of cycling in London: The impact of the 2007 Tour de France Grand Depart on the image and provision of cycling in the capital. *Journal of Sport & Tourism*, *17*(1), 43-61.

Abstract: There is a growing recognition of the importance of events in society and of the wide ranging impacts that are characterised through economic, tourism, political, social, environmental and cultural impacts. The reasons for staging events are many and varied. Two areas that have attracted research are the impact on the image of a host and the legacy of the event. Research demonstrates that staging an event can enhance the image of a host and that it can also act as catalyst for development. What is less clear from research though is how a host city uses an event to act as a catalyst for any kind of cultural or social change, since many events have limited impact beyond the immediate aftermath of their occurrence. The purpose of this paper is to explore how a host city might use a major event to enhance its image to an internal (as well as external) audience in order to subsequently promote specific social and cultural development and, in doing so, provide a platform for a meaningful legacy to the host community that extends beyond the immediacy of the actual event. The paper demonstrates how the image of London was enhanced by carefully selected promotional messages that, in turn, provided a basis for its reinvention as a cyclised city.

Keywords: Tour de France, event tourism, image enhancement, legacy, cycling provision

Discussion questions

How does stakeholder theory apply to the management of these types of planned event:
☐ Sports
☐ Festivals
☐ Business events
☐ Entertainment
☐ Mega events
☐ Hallmark events
☐ Iconic events

Assessment activities

Divide into groups in the class and choose three different forms of planned events where the bidding process was involved and the organizers were successful in their bids. Investigate how the processes were different and which aspects were more important for the different events.

Recommended additional readings and sources

Derrett, R. (2016). *The Complete Guide to Creating Enduring Festivals.* Hoboken, NJ: Wiley.

McGillivray, D. & Turner, D. (2018). *Event Bidding: Politics, Persuasion and Resistance.* London: Routledge.

References

Andersson, T. & Getz, D. (2008). Stakeholder management strategies of festivals. *Journal of Convention & Event Tourism*, **9**(3), 199-220.

Adongo, R. & Kim, S. (2018). The ties that bind: stakeholder collaboration and networking in local festivals. *International Journal of Contemporary Hospitality Management*, **30**(6), 2458-2480.

Adongo, R. (2017). Social exchange, collaboration, and networking between stakeholders in traditional festivals (Doctoral dissertation, The Hong Kong Polytechnic University).

Beek, R. & Go F. (2017). Legacy of hallmark events: Cross-cultural analysis among emerging destinations. In: Little, S., Go, F. & Poon, T.C. (eds), *Global Innovation and Entrepreneurship: Challenges and Experiences from East and West* (pp. 273–314). Cham, Switzerland: Palgrave Macmillan.

Berridge, G. (2012). The promotion of cycling in London: The impact of the 2007 Tour de France Grand Depart on the image and provision of cycling in the capital. *Journal of Sport & Tourism*, **17**(1), 43-61.

Bradish, C., & Cronin, J. J. (2009). Corporate social responsibility in sport. *Journal of Sport Management*, **23**(6), 691-697.

Brent Ritchie, J. R. (1984). Assessing the impact of hallmark events: Conceptual and research issues. *Journal of Travel Research*, **23**(1), 2-11.

Brannagan, P. M., & Rookwood, J. (2016). Sports mega-events, soft power and soft disempowerment: international supporters' perspectives on Qatar's acquisition of the 2022 FIFA World Cup finals. *International Journal of Sport Policy and Politics*, **8**(2), 173-188.

Bull, C. & Lovell, J. (2007). The impact of hosting major sporting events on local residents: An analysis of the views and perceptions of Canterbury residents in relation to the Tour de France 2007. *Journal of Sport & Tourism*, **12**(3-4), 229-248.

Buning, R. & Gibson, H. (2015). The evolution of active-sport-event travel careers. *Journal of Sport Management*, **29**, 555-569.

Buning, R. & Gibson, H. (2016). Exploring the trajectory of active-sport-event travel careers: A social worlds perspective. *Journal of Sport Management*, **30**, 265-281.

Chappelet, J. L. & Parent, M. M. (2015). The (Wide) World of Sports Events. Routledge Handbook of Sports Event Management, pp. 1-17.

Carlsen, J., Ali-Knight, J. & Robertson, M. (2007). Access—a research agenda for Edinburgh festivals. *Event Management*, **11**(1-2), 3-11.

Chi, C. G. Q., Ouyang, Z. & Xu, X. (2018). Changing perceptions and reasoning process: Comparison of residents' pre-and post-event attitudes. *Annals of Tourism Research*, **70**, 39-53.

Close, A. G., Lacey, R. & Cornwell, T. B. (2015). Visual Processing and need for cognition can enhance event-sponsorship outcomes: how sporting event sponsorships benefit from the way attendees process them. *Journal of Advertising Research*, **55**(2), 206-215.

Derrett, R. M. (2016). *The Complete Guide to Creating Enduring Festivals*. Hoboken, NJ: Wiley.

Emery, P. R. (2002). Bidding to host a major sports event: The local organising committee perspective. *International Journal of Public Sector Management*, **15**(4), 316-335.

Friedman, M, & Mason, D. (2004). A stakeholder approach to understanding economic development decision making: public subsidies for professional sport facilities. *Economic Development Quarterly*, **18**, 236-254.

Fotiadis, A. K., Vassiliadis, C. A. & Sotiriadis, M. D. (2016). The preferences of participants in small-scale sport events: A conjoint analysis case study from Taiwan. *Turizam: međunarodni znanstveno-stručni časopis*, **64**(2), 175-187.

Fotiadis, A., Xie, L., Li, Y. & Huan, T. C. T. (2016). Attracting athletes to small-scale sports events using motivational decision-making factors. *Journal of Business Research*, **69**(11), 5467-5472.

Frawley, S. (2015). Organizational power and the management of a mega-event: the case of Sydney 2000. *Event Management*, **19** (2), 247-260.

Gargalianos, D., Toohey, K. & Stotlar, D. (2015). Olympic Games complexity model (OGCM). *Event Management*, **19**, 47–55

Getz, D. (2004). Bidding on events: Identifying event selection criteria and critical success factors. In *Journal of Convention & Exhibition Management* 5, (2), 1-24).

Getz, D. (2013). *Event Tourism: Concepts, International Case Studies and Research*. Cognizant Communication Corporation.

Getz, D. & Andersson, T. (2008). Sustainable festivals: on becoming an institution. *Event Management*, **12** (1), 1-17.

Getz, D., Andersson, T. & Larson, M. (2006). Festival stakeholder roles: Concepts and case studies. *Event Management*, **10**(2-3), 103-122.

Getz, D. & Fairley, S. (2004). Media management at sport events for destination promotion: Case studies and concepts. *Event Management*, **8**, 127–139.

Getz, D., Svensson, B., Peterssen, R. & Gunnervall, A. (2012). Hallmark events: definition, goals and planning process. *International Journal of Event Management Research*, **7**, (1/2)

Hall, C. M. (1989). The definition and analysis of hallmark tourist events. *GeoJournal*, **19**(3), 263-268.

Hautbois, C., Parent, M. M. & Séguin, B. (2012). How to win a bid for major sporting events? A stakeholder analysis of the 2018 Olympic Winter Games French bid. *Sport Management Review*, **15**(3), 263-275.

Hjalager, A. M. & Kwiatkowski, G. (2017). Entrepreneurial implications, prospects and dilemmas in rural festivals. *Journal of Rural Studies*, **63**, 217-228.

Horbel, C., Popp, B. Woratschek, H. & Wilson, B. (2016). How context shapes value co-creation: spectator experience of sport events. *Service Industries Journal*, **36**(11-12), 510-531.

Kim, S. S. & Petrick, J. F. (2005). Residents' perceptions on impacts of the FIFA 2002 World Cup: the case of Seoul as a host city. *Tourism Management*, **26**(1), 25-38.

Knott, B., Fyall, A. & Jones, I. (2015). The nation branding opportunities provided by a sport mega-event: South Africa and the 2010 FIFA World Cup. *Journal of Destination Marketing & Management*, **4**(1), 46-56.

Ko, Y. J., Chang, Y., Park, C. & Herbst, F. (2017). Determinants of consumer attitude toward corporate sponsors: A comparison between a profit and nonprofit sport event sponsorship. *Journal of Consumer Behaviour*, **16**(2), 176-186.

Larson, M. (2002). A political approach to relationship marketing: Case study of the Storsjöyran Festival. *International Journal of Tourism Research*, **4**(2), 119-143.

Larson, M. (2009). Joint event production in the jungle, the park, and the garden: Metaphors of event networks. *Tourism Management*, **30**(3), 393-399.

Larson, M. & Wikström, E. (2001). Organizing events: Managing conflict and consensus in a political market square. *Event Management*, **7**(1), 51-65.

Levy, P. (2007). *Iconic Events: Media, Politics, and Power in Retelling History*, Lexicon Books, Lanham. MD.

Lockstone-Binney, L., Whitelaw, P., Robertson, M., Junek, O. & Michael, I. (2014). The motives of ambassadors in bidding for international association meetings and events. *Event Management*, **18**(1), 65-74.

Mackellar, J. (2015). Determinants of business engagement with regional sport events. *European Sport Management Quarterly*, **15**(1), 7-26.

Mackellar, J. (2006). Conventions, festivals, and tourism: Exploring the network that binds. *Journal of Convention and Event Tourism*, 8 (2), 45-56.

Misener, L. & Mason, D. (2006). Creating community networks: Can sporting events offer meaningful sources of social capital? *Managing Leisure*, **11**, 39–56.

Misener, L., Taks, M., Chalip, L. & Green, B. C. (2015). The elusive 'trickle-down effect' of sport events: Assumptions and missed opportunities. *Managing Sport and Leisure*, **20**(2), 135-156.

Mitchell, R., Agle, B.R. & Wood, D.J. (1997). Toward a theory of stakeholder identification and salience: defining the principle of who and what really counts. *Academy of Management Review*, **22** (4): 853–886.

Moital, I., Jackson, C. & Le Couillard, J. (2013). Using scenarios to investigate stakeholders' views on the future of a sporting event. *Event Management*, **17**, (4), 439-452.

Morla, D. & Ladkin, A. (2006). The convention industry in Galicia and Santiago de Compostela: Stakeholder perceptions of its success and potential for growth. *Event Management*, **10** (4), 241-251.

Müller, M. (2015). What makes an event a mega-event? Definitions and sizes. *Leisure Studies*, **34**(6), 627-642.

Nordvall, A. & Heldt, T. (2017). Understanding hallmark event failure: a case study of a Swedish music festival. *International Journal of Event and Festival Management*, **8**(2), 172-185.

Numerato, D. (2015). Who says 'no' to modern football? Italian supporters, reflexivity, and neo-liberalism. *Journal of Sport and Social Issues*, **39**(2), 120-138.

Parent, M., & Séguin, B. (2007). Factors that led to the drowning of a world championship organizing committee: A stakeholder approach. *European Sport Management Quarterly*, **7**(2), 187-212.

Parent, M. & Slack, T. (2007). Conformity and resistance: Preparing a Francophone sporting event in North America. *Event Management*, **11**(3), 129-143.

Preuss, H. & Alfs, C. (2011) Signaling through the 2008 Beijing Olympics—using mega sport events to change the perception and image of the host, *European Sport Management Quarterly*, **11**(1), 55-71

Ramchandani, G., Coleman, R. J. & Bingham, J. (2017). Sport participation behaviours of spectators attending major sports events and event induced attitudinal changes towards sport. *International Journal of Event and Festival Management*, **8**(2), 121-135.

Ritchie, J. B. & Beliveau, D. (1974). Hallmark events: An evaluation of a strategic response to seasonality in the travel market. *Journal of Travel Research*, **13**(2), 14-20.

Sadd, D. (2010). What is event-led regeneration? Are we confusing terminology or will London 2012 be the first games to truly benefit the local existing population? *Event Management*, **13**, 265–275.

Scheinbaum, A. C. & Lacey, R. (2015). Event social responsibility: A note to improve outcomes for sponsors and events. *Journal of Business Research*, **68**(9), 1982-1986.

Taks, M., Green, B. C., Misener, L. & Chalip, L. (2018). Sport participation from sport events: why it doesn't happen?. *Marketing Intelligence & Planning*, **36**(2), 185-198.

Todd, L., Leask, A. & Ensor, J. (2017). Understanding primary stakeholders' multiple roles in hallmark event tourism management. *Tourism Management*, **59**, 494-509.

Turco, D. M. (2015). The influence of sponsorship on product recall and image among sport spectators. In *Proceedings of the 1995 World Marketing Congress* (pp. 8-12). Springer, Cham.

Vilkas, Á. & Wada, E. (2017). Hospitality and stakeholders in events. Multiple case study in Florianópolis, Santa Catarina, Brazil. *Revista Turismo & Desenvolvimento*, **27/28** (1), 217-228.

Walters, G., & Tacon, R. (2010). Corporate social responsibility in sport: Stakeholder management in the UK football industry. *Journal of Management & Organization*, **16**(4), 566-586.

6 Stakeholder Considerations for Residents, Communities and Cities

Learning objectives

At the end of the chapter readers should be able to:

☐ Define event tourism, place identity, place attachment and tourist destination

☐ Identify the most important aspects to consider for residents' engagement

☐ Understand the needs of the community

☐ Apply stakeholder theory to the city

6.1 Introduction

Events, and therefore event tourism, tend to be attached to their host communities, even embedded within close and strong stakeholder networks. It is true there are many footloose events, won through bidding, or otherwise moving around the world, but a degree of dependence on place and social networks is the norm. This raises two concepts of importance: place identity and place attachment. This chapter will focus on the aspects that are important for the residents during stakeholder engagement. It will also look at the needs of the community and apply the stakeholder theory to the city and destination.

6.2 Key terms defined

Event tourism

"Event tourism at the city or destination level is the development and marketing of planned events as tourist attractions, catalysts, animators, image makers and place makers. This process includes bidding on, facilitating and creating events, and the management of portfolios of events as destination assets" Getz, 2013.

Place identity and events

" Events and other planned events can foster and reinforce group identity" Getz, 2013.

Place attachment and events

" Events are connected to cultures and to places, giving each identify and helping bind people to their communities" Getz, 2013.

Place making

Richards and Palmer (2010, pp. 418-19) argue for place making, rather than place marketing, in the context of their treatise on 'Eventful Cities'. They explained that creating a sense of place can be facilitated through events by stressing distinctiveness of the environment, promoting festivity, developing event spaces and a festival community and creating new rhythms of everyday life. This gives a unique identity to places and encourages residents to feel attachment to their communities.

Tourist destination

A tourist destination consists of the network of government agencies, marketing organizations, services, and attractions that collaborate to attract and serve the needs of visitors.

6.3 Case Study: Cappadox 2018, Turkey

Bekir Bora Dedeoğlu – Nevsehir HBV University Turkey

Cappadox was first organized in 2015. This festival is held every year and embodies various activities ranging from music, contemporary art, gastronomy and open-air programs. Within the scope of the music programs various singers perform while exhibitions are held in the form of contemporary art programs, and also trekkings, trips and tours are organized. As a part of gastronomy program, gourmet delicacies are tried and picnics are organized. On the other hand, trekking, yoga and nightwatching activities are arranged for the open-air program. Each year Cappadox is organized with a different theme. The theme was 'Cappadocia Struck' in 2015, 'Let Us Cultivate Our Garden' in 2016, 'Ways Out From The World' in 2017 and 'Silence' in 2018 (Cappadox, 2018). The number of days and people joining the festival increase every year.

While it took three days in 2015, four days were allocated in 2016 and 2017, and it was extended to six days in 2018. The number of people joining Cappadox was six thousand in 2016; however, it reached up to ten thousand people in 2017 (Laleli, 2017). In addition, Cappadox is considered by Conde Nast Traveller as one of the best festivals in the world (Conde Nast Traveller, 2018).

Questions

Who are the stakeholders involved in the organization of the festival Cappadox?

Cappadox is an activity organized by Pozitif. Therefore, all team members working in Pozitif are the stakeholders of this organization. Besides Pozitif, local firms and agencies are among the important stakeholders. Since Cappadox is organized based on four main programs of music, contemporary art, gastronomy and open-air, we have different stakeholders as academicians, artists and members of the chamber of commerce who contribute to the organization, development and implementation stages of every program. Activities in each program are carried out in different regions and avenues, local people and local firms are among our stakeholders, as well. Despite the fact that it does not fit into your definition, Cappadocia, in our opinion, is the most powerful stakeholder with its unique atmosphere, historical background and cultural structure.

What kind of process have you been through to define your stakeholders? What were the criteria you used for choosing your stakeholders?

Since Pozitif is an organization possessing the purposes of providing entertaining and leading experiences, we wanted to maintain the same philosophy while organizing the Cappadox. Therefore, the point we paid the highest attention was to mirroring the philosophy and sensations of Cappadox. We tried to choose our stakeholders, accordingly.

Cappadox is built on four main programs. For this reason, we paid special attention to work with individuals and groups with relevant expertise. Furthermore, we cared about choosing our stakeholders from individuals experienced at recreational activities as much as possible.

Was one stakeholder group in the festival more important than the other stakeholder group? Why?

Due to its multidisciplinary nature, Cappadox embodies various stakeholder groups. It focuses on four main disciplines: Music, Contemporary Art, Gastronomy and Open Air. All these disciplines have their own stakeholders. It would not be right to indicate that one group was more important than the other one. We cannot even say that different stakeholders in one discipline occupy a more important position than others. For instance, for the organization of any musical activity, many stakeholders ranging from orchestra, those responsible for concert area to those responsible for meeting the needs of audience. Putting these stakeholders in an order of importance would not be fair because it would not be possible to talk about successful events

Photos 6.1 to 6.4: Cappadox. Picture credit: B. B. Dedeoğlu

without the contribution of each stakeholder. Therefore, all stakeholders are evenly important. Although Cappadox includes four programs, music programs have special place within the whole festival program in terms of the attractiveness of the festival. Therefore, stakeholders involved in music program could be considered as a little bit more important.

How did you invite stakeholders to the festival?

Cappadox is a different festival due to the organized activities. We invite all stakeholders with the intention of ensuring their contribution to the development and enrichment of the contents of four different festival areas.

Have you ever faced a problem with stakeholders? If so, could you tell something about it?

Cappadox embodies many programs. Although we communicate information about the programs, our guests might feel unsatisfied due to lack of information about the starting time and avenues of activities included in the program. Besides, all guests have different expectations therefore some might find activities not good enough to satisfy their expectations. However, we should indicate that many of our guests are happy with the festival. As one of our most important stakeholders, local people complain about the problems caused by the crowd. Traffic congestion and parking problems are the main problems. Despite the fact that Cappadox has unique cultural value in the field of gastronomy, our guests sometimes damage the Cappadocia region which has a peculiar nature, which raises negative reactions in local people.

What kind of problems did you face with your stakeholders at all stages of Cappadox?

The main aim of firms joining the festival is to get economic profit. Due to different programs in Cappadox, some firms could get less profit than others. This kind of matters does not fall into our responsibility area; however, we could hear specific criticisms from stakeholders regarding the unsuccessful management of the organization.

Were there special activities for local people of the region where the festival was organized?

Since the activities in Cappadox are carried out in different regions and avenues, local people can benefit from its cultural and economic outputs. Especially within the scope of gastronomy program, the promotion of local food is prioritized.

During the stages of Cappadox festival, how did you manage all your stakeholders?

The prerequisite of a successful organization is ensuring the coordination. Therefore, special attention was put on the coordination between stakeholders. Responsible persons were selected for each program and they ensured the coordination. But before ensuring the coordination, it was aimed that all stakeholders become aware of the philosophy of the work they carry out. For this reason, necessary information is provided on the main purpose of the activity before inviting stakeholders to an activity raising positive sensations in general.

What are the acquisitions you got / the lessons learnt from the cooperation/partnership with stakeholders?

Partnerships provided us with different perspectives. Especially the feedbacks from guests will help us take the necessary steps to make Cappadox more exciting and a desired activity. Those feedbacks will also enable us to decide what to offer and be more innovative during the activities to be organized in Cappadox. Furthermore, we have become more aware of the steps to be taken in order to minimize the problems faced by local people. We need to improve our collaboration with state institutions to be able to eliminate the complaints of local people.

Discussion

It should also not be overlooked that the activities on the music program are in the forefront, although it is stated that all stakeholders are valued equally. As mentioned by Menon and Levitin (2005), music is a part of most people's lives. For this reason, singers and groups who will attract the interests of individuals at the festival may be important in terms of their participation in the festival. Indeed, as emphasized by Packer and Ballantyne (2011), experiencing live music performance is a very important factor for guests.

Although there are no major problems in the event, local residents and guests have minor problems. While local people faces problems in terms of traffic congestion and parking problems, it can be said that some of the guests are experiencing problems due to lack of information about the festival. Although the organizers do not perform local community-based activities, they state that the festival is a serious socio-cultural benefit to the local people. This finding is consistent with Gursoy et al. (2004). According to Gursoy et al. (2004), organizers believe that festivals and events provide more social benefits to local people than cost. In this study, the organizers also think that the festival benefits local people in terms of socio-cultural. However, organizers are aware that local people are experiencing problems such as traffic congestion and lack of parking. For this reason, they plan to develop solutions for these problems in the future.

In order for the festival to be successful, organizers attach importance to coordination among stakeholders. For this reason, each program is implemented by its own responsible managers. As noted by Donner et al. (2014), coordination is one of the most important aspects of the successful branding of a product with multiple stakeholders. At this point it can be stated that coordination is important so that festivals that come from such multiple stakeholders can be successful.

6.4 Residents (the host community)

One of the foundation principles of stakeholder theory is that those who affect and can be affected by the focal organization have legitimate claims to be consulted or involved. No group is more deserving of key stakeholder status than residents, as in the world of events they are the source of consumer demand, volunteer support and political influence on the one hand, and are the most impacted group, directly or indirectly, by events and tourism. Failure to inform, consult and involve the host community is undoubtedly a recipe for problems, if not disaster, as witnessed by many events that have withered or been terminated because of their poor relations or bad image within a community. And certainly a failure to secure adequate resources, the most common direct reason for failure, is at least partially attributable to not possessing strong stakeholder support.

The interesting thing about residents, as a stakeholder group (or constituency) is that their needs and interests transcend the full spectrum of interests by all the other possible stakeholder categories. Figure: 6.1 illustrates this thesis, showing how the needs (or demands or wants) of residents will emerge through health agencies, sports clubs and teams, parks and recreation, arts and culture, green cities and environmental lobbies, the private sector and jobs, and of course local/regional government and politics. So if 'residents' or the 'community' is the number one salient stakeholder group, it can be either approached through all the clubs, institutions, agencies and companies based in the area, or through omnibus resident surveys and consultation mechanisms. A big job!

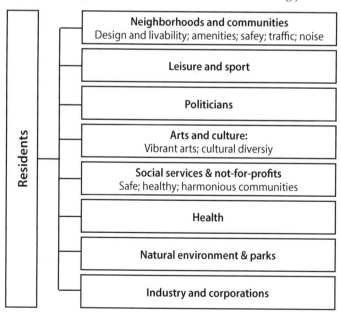

Figure 6.1: Residents and their needs. Adapted from Getz (2016).

There is quite a lot of literature on community impacts and the effects of events on residents in general, but most of it does not relate explicitly to stakeholder management. A starting point is to recognize that community or resident needs and wants are not homogeneous. The diagram shows a number of stakeholder categories that often are organized as lobby groups (or at least have identifiable spokespeople), but these are also all of interest to the community at large – including the industry and corporate perspectives, as that is where jobs are created. In addition, residents frequently organize around issues that affect the places in which they live, giving rise to the 'not in my backyard' syndrome.

For many events the most important supporter and regulator is the local authority or municipality (van Niekerk, 2014, Witford, 2004). From the perspective of local government, events fulfill diverse and important roles, and over the past several decades events have come to occupy a prominent and sometimes central place in community and urban policies. This trend is documented in the book *Eventful Cities* (Richards and Palmer, 2010).

Politicians speak for residents, especially if they are elected at the level of neighborhood or community, but they do not always reflect the range of values and opinions found in their wards. In good governance of a city or nation, elected officials cannot simply bow to pressure from lobbyists or take parochial positions on all issues; they have to represent the whole.

Research notes

Van Niekerk, M. (2014). The role of the public sector in tourism destination management from a network relationship approach. *Tourism Analysis*, **19**, 701–718.

Abstract: The study aims to determine the suitability of the dyadic approach and the network relationship approach when engaging destination stakeholders and to identify the roles of the public sector within destination management. These study aims are investigated in the context of Mbombela Local Municipality, South Africa. A conceptual framework was developed based on a literature review. Data were then collected through official documents, 55 semi-structured interviews with key stakeholders, a local economic summit, forum discussions, and 504 demand- and 403 supply-side questionnaires. The study findings suggest that the network relationship approach was the most suitable approach for the engagement of destination stakeholders. In addition to the roles identified in previous studies, the study findings identified several additional roles that the public sector should fulfill in destination management. Based on the study findings, a new conceptual framework for the role of the public sector in destination management has been proposed. By utilizing the conceptual framework developed in this study, destinations can engage their stakeholders more effectively and increase the attractiveness of their destinations. This is one of a few studies from Africa providing empirical findings on destination management and the role of the public sector within destination management.

Keywords: Destination management, roles of public sector, network relationship approach, stakeholder theory

Whitford, M. (2004). Event public policy development in the Northern Sub-Regional Organization of Councils, Queensland Australia: Rhetoric or realization? *Journal of Convention and Event Tourism*, **6**(3), 81–99.

Abstract: Over the last two decades, Australia has witnessed the emergence of a socially and economically significant event industry with an increasingly professional profile. Many governments, as stakeholders in the development of events, have produced policies designed to facilitate the growth and potential of events as a platform for industry and economic development (Burgan and Mules, 2000). Thus, events are increasingly becoming an integral and essential component of regional development. The purpose of this qualitative study was to analyze and evaluate public policies pertaining to events produced from 1980 to 2002 by the Northern Sub-Regional Organization of Councils (NORSROC) located in South East Queensland's Sunshine Coast, Australia.

The seven NORSROC local governments are situated in and around the tourist region of the Sunshine Coast of Queensland. The results of analysis revealed NORSROC members, over a twenty-two year period, produced a scant number of non-specific event policies that were developed in what appeared to be a small and potentially insular event policy community. Furthermore, NORSROC public policies appeared to give little recognition to events as a vehicle to facilitate entrepreneurial enterprises and/or regional development. Arguably, the sustainability of events in the region will be severely curtailed if NORSROC members do not adopt a more whole of government, proactive entrepreneurial approach to the development of event public policy so they can ensure in future years, they have "something to offer everyone" (Touring the Sunshine Coast, 2003, p. 1).

Keywords: Australian local government, public policy, events, content analysis, policy community

Reid, S. (2011). Event stakeholder management: Developing sustainable rural event practices. *International Journal of Event and Festival Management*, **2** (1), 20-36.

Abstract: *Purpose*: Changes to the economic and social fabric of rural communities in Australia have resulted in an outmigration of residents, shifting economies and disenfranchisement with rural life styles. As a result, events provide important social and recreational opportunities for residents. However, rural communities are constrained by limited resources, such as the number of individuals who are willing and able to participate in event organizations; therefore, it is essential for the sustainable organization of events that stakeholders are attracted and retained. This paper aims to apply a stakeholder theoretical approach to the organizing and planning of rural events to identify event stakeholders, monitor satisfaction and ensure stakeholder retention within rural events.

Design/methodology/approach: A qualitative research design using a multiple case study approach examined event stakeholders in three rural communities of Southwest Queensland, Australia. In total, 54 in-depth interviews were undertaken with event stakeholders and analyzed using an iterative thematic content analysis.

Findings: The findings reveal that rural-event stakeholders fulfill multiple roles, differentiated by risk, and fraught with competing or conflicting agendas. The paper identifies strategies that event organizers utilize to manage relationships, and that facilitate stakeholder satisfaction and continued involvement.

Originality/value: There is limited understanding of event stakeholders, particularly in rural communities. Involving rural residents in organizing and planning events develops individual skills, knowledge and capacity. Rural communities benefit from an ability to deal with adverse conditions based on improvements in capacity of individuals and the community.

Keywords: Rural areas, stakeholder analysis, Australia, event management

Reid, S. (2007). Identifying social consequences of rural events. *Event Management*, **11** (1/2), 89-98.

Abstract: Events have a range of consequences for host communities. While a number of researchers have focused upon impact assessment, there are some fundamental issues that require addressing. First, most research investigating the social impacts of events use predefined quantitative assessment techniques or tools. These tools limit the ability of respondents to indicate the diversity of social consequences that they may experience. Second, the labeling of social consequences as positive or negative fails to acknowledge the 'shades of gray' that may exist. Third, there is a lack of research specifically investigating the social consequences of events within rural communities. Therefore, there is a need to identify a range of social consequences that occur as a result of hosting events, especially within rural communities. This is best achieved from the perspective of those experiencing the phenomena, thus qualitatively. This article aims to address these gaps by examining the social consequences of rural events from an event stakeholder perspective within three rural communities of Southwest Queensland, Australia. Specifically, this article reports on a number of social consequences identified that have been underutilized or discussed within the existing literature.

Keywords: Social consequences; rural events

6.5 Cities/destinations

Destinations can be defined in many ways, such as by reference to tourist image or origin-destination analysis, by calling cities and resorts destinations, by simply using government jurisdictions and of course by reference to the work of DMOs. But here is one that is especially formulated for this book: *"A tourist destination consists of the network of government agencies, marketing organizations, services, and attractions that collaborate to attract and serve the needs of visitors."* A number of researchers have pointed to the vital role of networks and collaboration in making tourism destinations function, such as the paper by Framke.

Research notes

Framke, W. (2002). The destination as a concept: A discussion of the business-related perspective versus the socio-cultural approach in tourism theory. *Scandinavian Journal of Hospitality and Tourism*, 2(2), 92-108.

Abstract: This article investigates the use of the concept destination in selected economically and socio-culturally-oriented tourism textbooks, monographs and anthologies. It proposes that there are different understandings of the concept destination. Destinations are seen as units at several geographical levels, but without distinct geographical boundaries, and as images resulting from social practice. The content of the destination is seen on the one hand as an agglomeration of attractions and services, and on the other as a dynamic agglomeration of attractions, culture, events, landscapes and services. Economic writers have an implicit understanding of the need for cooperation among the actors at a destination, while socio-cultural authors emphasize unspecified connections and social practice. Finally, the tourist is characterized either as an economic consumer or as an experience-seeking social actor and consumer.

Keywords: Cooperation, destination boundaries, destination content, tourist behaviour

Merrilees, B., Getz, D. & O'Brien, D. (2005). Marketing stakeholder analysis. Branding the Brisbane Goodwill Games. *European Journal of Marketing*, 39 (9/10), 1060-1077.

Abstract: *Purpose:* The paper aims to explore a major issue in international marketing: how to build a global brand in a way that makes a strong local connection.

Design/methodology/approach: Using qualitative research methods on a single case, the Brisbane Goodwill Games, the processes used in the staging of this major sport event are analyzed. In particular, the stakeholder relations employed by the marketing department of the Goodwill Games Organization are investigated and a process model is developed that explains how a global brand can be built locally.

Findings: A major outcome of the paper is a revision to the four-step Freeman process to make it more proactive; and three major principles for effective stakeholder management are articulated. The findings demonstrate that stakeholder analysis and management can be used to build more effective event brands. Stakeholder theory is also proposed as an appropriate and possibly stronger method of building inter-organizational linkages than alternatives such as network theory.

Originality/value: Previous literature has generally dealt with the global brand issue in terms of the standardization versus adaptation debate, and the extent to which the marketing mix should be adapted to meet local needs in foreign countries. This research provides a unique extension to this literature by demonstrating how the brand itself needs to be modified to meet local needs.

Keywords: Brands, international marketing, stakeholder analysis, research paper

Ford, R., Peeper, W. & Gresock, A. (2009). Friends to grow and foes to know: Using a stakeholder matrix to identify management strategies for convention and visitor bureaus. *Journal of Convention & Event Tourism,* **10** (3), 166-184

Abstract: Effective stakeholder management is essential in today's dynamic business environment, especially in the case of convention and visitor bureaus that are dependent upon destination stakeholder support for critical resources. This article uses the resource-dependency theory to propose a typology for strategically managing stakeholders using convention and visitors' bureaus as a case example. Building on previous research, it offers a new focus and categorization using both control over resources and mission congruence to help executives strategically manages their stakeholders and achieve their mission. By analyzing how different stakeholders can be considered friends, foes, or neutrals, strategies are offered that convention and visitors bureaus, destination marketing organizations, and other organizations can use to manage multiple stakeholders. The framework presented also serves as a basis for empirical work with the potential to inform theory and practice.

Keywords: resource dependency, stakeholder, convention and visitors' bureaus, destination-marketing organizations

With this definition it can be a city, resort, region or country, and more importantly it can be a viewed as a nested hierarchy, as illustrated below.

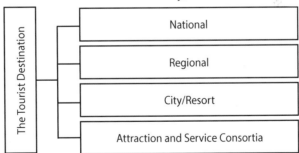

Figure 6.2: The tourist destination as a hierarchy of stakeholder networks

Several principles can be stated that reinforce the stakeholder perspective on destinations.

♦ **Principle 1:** Tourist destinations require, and can be defined by the stakeholder networks that attract and serve visitors. Destination networks can overlap in terms of geographic coverage, target markets, and permanent or temporary consortia.

Residents generally do not think of themselves as living in a tourist destination, although clearly the residents of resorts know how important tourism is, and probably are familiar with the roles of their DMO. The more important tourism becomes, the more residents will likely demand to be fully involved, not just informed. This leads to Principle 2.

♦ **Principle 2:** Tourist destinations should implement community-based planning entailing full resident and multi-stakeholder engagement.

Community-based tourism planning became popular in the 1980s, particularly with the publication of Murphy's book in 1985: *Tourism: A Community Approach*. Hall's approach to event planning, as articulated in the 1992 book *Hallmark Tourist Events* advocated participatory planning. From an earlier article by Hall (1989, pp. 33-4): "*...community involvement encourages greater variation and local flavor in the nature of the event and the tourist destination, assists in the protection of the tourist resources, and reduces opposition to tourist development.*" Most tourism and event planning literature recognizes the importance of wide consultations and consideration of multiple perspectives. Getz, in the book *Festivals, Special Events and Tourism* (1991: 140), explicitly referred to "stakeholder input" in his destination planning model for event tourism, and discussed "public forums and stakeholder surveys" as input to event evaluation and impact assessment. The Fredline & Faulkner paper demonstrates the necessity of public participation and how perceptions and attitudes can be measured. Subsequently social impact assessment has been an important theme in the events literature.

♦ **Principle 3:** Destination stakeholder networks can be situational or issue-specific.

The third principle recognizes that collaborative networks are not only dynamic but they can form and re-form around specific situations (such as the area affected by an event) or issues (e.g., the need for new infrastructure). In the Alonso article the network relates to a food and wine event, but with implications for destination marketing.

Research notes

Duarte Alonso, A. (2016). Stakeholders, collaboration, food, and wine: The case of Jumilla's Gastronomic Days. *Journal of Convention & Event Tourism* **17**(3), 173-191.

Abstract: An emerging literature on gastronomic events highlights the growing interest among academics, event organizers, and development agencies in identifying potential or actual outcomes from gastronomic events. Partly in response to such interest, this study seeks to contribute to the literature on events management, studying the contribution of various stakeholders involved in the 'Gastronomic Days' of Jumilla, Spain. Semi-structured, face-to-face, in depth interviews were conducted with the managers and owners of four participating businesses to the event. The data collection was complemented through on-site visits, observations, and interviews with eight other local businesses. The findings underline the significance of collaboration among these participants to grow and sustain the event, as well as voluntary efforts by event stakeholders. Importantly, a common objective was identified in the form of enhancing the image of the local products, and overall that of the region, to 'convert' residents, and also outside consumers and tourists to Jumilla's products. These findings have significant implications for Jumilla's community. In particular, the importance and efforts of a region's food stakeholders in contributing to adding value and improving the local food culture emerge as useful aspects, with potential benefits for local food growers, hospitality and tourism sectors, and residents.

Keywords: Collaboration, gastronomic events, Jumilla, Spain, stakeholders, stakeholder theory, triple bottom line

Stokes, R. (2008). Tourism strategy making: Insights to the events tourism domain. *Tourism Management*, **29**, 252–262.

Abstract: This research examines the strategy concept (Hax & Majluf, 1991) in tourism before exploring how different schools of strategy (Mintzberg, 1994) are applied in events tourism. It then investigates the stakeholder orientations of strategy makers in this domain. While reference to tourism planning is long-standing, 'tourism strategy' is often submerged in discussions of destination management and marketing. For this study, a two-step, qualitative methodology involving convergent interviews (Dick, 1990). and multiple case research (Yin, 1993, 1994) across six Australian states/ territories was adopted. Findings show that events tourism strategies of public sector events agencies (within or outside tourism bodies) are mostly reactive or proactive relative to emerging episodes/events. Among three strategy-making frameworks that reflect different stakeholder orientations, a corporate, market-led framework with limited stakeholder engagement was more prevalent than the community, destination-led or synergistic frameworks for strategy making.

Keywords: Tourism strategy; events tourism; stakeholder orientation

Stokes, R. (2007). Relationships and networks for shaping events tourism: An Australian study. *Event Management*, **10**, 145–158

Abstract: This article shows how convergent interviews were used to identify themes and issues and refine a theoretical framework for multiple case research in the events tourism domain. In particular, the research examined how and why interorganizational relationships of public sector events development agencies impact upon events tourism strategy making in Australia. The body of knowledge about interorganizational relationships and networks and tourism strategies, including events tourism, provided the platform to study four research issues. Findings showed that the public sector environment, a diversity of strategy forms and processes, a range of network and relationship characteristics, and incentives and disincentives for using networks in strategy making were valuable themes to investigate in the case research.

Keywords: Interorganizational relationships, networks, events tourism, Australia

Discussion questions

1   Define event tourism and tourist destination
2   Explain how events can contribute to place making
3   Identify the most important aspects to consider for the engagement of residents
4   What research would you do to understand the needs of the community?
5   When applying stakeholder theory to the city or community, who would you consult and why?

Assessment activities

The community is a very important stakeholder specifically when it comes to city events. Divide into groups and choose one city event in your area. Interview the organizer of the event and compile a report by asking him/her the following questions. How did the organizers of a city event in your area involve the community? What were some of the benefits that the community received before, during and after the event? Bring the report back to class and share with other groups.

Recommended readings and additional sources

Getz, D. (2013). *Event Tourism: Concepts, International Case Studies, and Research.* New York: Cognizant Communications.

References

Cappadox (2018). About Cappadox. http://cappadox.com/about-cappadox/cappadoxen. Last accessed: 08.09.2018.

Conde Nast Traveller (2018). The best festivals in the World for 2018. https://www.cntraveller.com/gallery/best-festivals. Last accessed: 08.09.2018

Dick, B. (1990). *Convergent Interviewing* (3rd ed.). Chapel Hill, Queensland: Interchange

Duarte Alonso, A. (2016, July). Stakeholders, collaboration, food, and wine: The case of Jumilla's Gastronomic Days. *Journal of Convention & Event Tourism* **17**, (3), 173-191.

Ford, R., Peeper, W., & Gresock, A. (2009). Friends to grow and foes to know: using a stakeholder matrix to identify management strategies for convention and visitor bureaus. *Journal of Convention & Event Tourism*, **10**(3), 166-184

Framke, W. (2002). The destination as a concept: A discussion of the business-related perspective versus the socio-cultural approach in tourism theory. *Scandinavian Journal of Hospitality and Tourism*, **2**(2), 92-108.

Getz, D. (1991). *Festivals,Special Events, and Tourism*. Van Nostrand Reinhold.

Getz, D. (2013). *Event Tourism: Concepts, International Case Studies and Research*. Cognizant Communication Corporation.

Gursoy, D., Kim, K. & Uysal, M. (2004). Perceived impacts of festivals and special events by organizers: an extension and validation. *Tourism Management*, **25**(2), 171-181.

Hall, C. M. (1989). The definition and analysis of hallmark tourist events. *GeoJournal*, **19**(3), 263-268.

Hall, C.M. (1992). *Hallmark Tourist Events: Impacts, Management and Planning*. London: Belhaven.

Hax, A., Majluf, N. (1991). *The Strategy Concept and Process: A Pragmatic Approach*. Englewood Cliffs, NJ: Prentice-Hall International

Menon, V. & Levitin, D. J. (2005). The rewards of music listening: response and physiological connectivity of the mesolimbic system. *Neuroimage*, **28**(1), 175-184.

Merrilees, B., Getz, D. & O'Brien, D. (2005). Marketing stakeholder analysis. Branding the Brisbane Goodwill Games. *European Journal of Marketing*, **39** (9/10), 1060-1077.

Mintzberg, H. (1994). *The Rise and Fall of Strategic Planning*. New York: Prentice-Hall

Murphy, P. (1985). *Tourism: A Community Approach*. New York: Methuen.

Packer, J. & Ballantyne, J. (2011). The impact of music festival attendance on young people's psychological and social well-being. *Psychology of Music*, **39**(2), 164-181.

Reid, S. (2007). Identifying social consequences of rural events. *Event Management*, **11**(1/2), 89-98.

Reid, S. (2011). Event stakeholder management: Developing sustainable rural event practices. *International Journal of Event and Festival Management*, **2**(1), 20-36.

Richards, G. & Palmer, R. (2010). *Eventful Cities: Cultural Management and Urban Regeneration*. A Butterworth-Heinemann Title

Stokes, R. (2008). Tourism strategy making: Insights to the events tourism domain. *Tourism Management*, **29**, 252–262.

Stokes, R. (2007). Relationships and networks for shaping events tourism: An Australian study. *Event Management*, **10**, 145–158

Van Niekerk, M. (2014). The role of the public sector in tourism destination management from a network relationship approach. *Tourism Analysis*, **19**(6), 701-718.

Whitford, M. (2004). Event public policy development in the Northern Sub-Regional Organization of Councils, Queensland Australia: Rhetoric or realization? *Journal of Convention and Event Tourism, 6*(3), 81–99.

Yin, R.K. (1993). *Applications of Case Study Research.* (revised ed., Vol. 5) Newbury Park, CA: Sage Publications

Yin, R.K. (1994). *Case Study Research: Design and methods.* (2nd ed., Vol. 5) Thousand Oaks, CA: Sage Publications

Index

Printed in the United States
By Bookmasters